Taxmageddon 2018:
How to Brace for the Trump Tax Plan

DIANE KENNEDY, CPA

Copyright © 2018 Diane Kennedy, CPA
All rights reserved.
ISBN: 978-1-949493-00-9

Acknowledgements

You can't build a business, or a book, without a team. I'm grateful for the team I have that supports me with my writing, my websites and my business.

Huge thanks for the support and expertise they provide to Jorge Manzitti, Saira Hameed and Rebecca Woodward. "Taxmageddon 2018: How to Brace for the Trump Tax Plan" wouldn't have existed without your help.

Thank you for being part of our CPA business team: Adriana Martinez, Bruce Warner, Oscar Friedman, Barbara Diederich and Flerida St Aubin.

Thank you for the excellent branding, business and marketing help, Shane Hunter.

And, of course, a huge thank you to my husband, Richard Cooley. You've always got my back. In an uncertain world, being able to count on someone else is a powerful thing.

Contents

Disclaimer iv

Introduction 5

Section I: Tax Act Strategies for Your Personal Return 7

Chapter 1: The Standard Deduction Vs Itemizing 8

Chapter 2: The Loss of Miscellaneous Deductions 22

Chapter 3: Strategies for Your Personal Residence 33

Chapter 4: Dependent Deductions 44

Chapter 5: Individual & Investment Tax Strategies for 2018 & Beyond 49

Section II: Start a Business 57

Chapter 6: Why Start a Business? 58

Chapter 7: Sure You Think You Have a Business, But Does the IRS Agree? 67

Chapter 8: The Best Business to Start 77

Chapter 9: Business Tax Basics Everyone Forgets 83

Section III: Strategic Business Tax Changes 109

Chapter 10: Pass-Through Entity Income Reduction 110

Chapter 11: More Business Strategies and Changes 127

Chapter 12: C Corporations and the Tax Cuts and Jobs Act 136

Chapter 13: Avoid C Corporation Traps 149

Chapter 14: Real Estate Investor Changes in Tax Cuts & Jobs Act 168

Section 4: Put Your Plan in Action 178

Chapter 15: What Will You Do Now? 179

Chapter 16: The Last Inch 190

Disclaimer
Information Only – Not Legal Advice

This publication is designed to provide general information regarding the subject matter covered. It is not intended to serve as legal, tax, or other financial advice related to individual situations. Each individual's legal, tax, and financial situation is different. For this reason, you are advised to consult with us, your own attorney, CPA, and/or other advisor regarding your specific situation.

The information and all accompanying material are for your use and convenience only. We have taken reasonable precautions in the preparation of this material and believe that the information presented here is accurate as of the date it was written. However, we will assume no responsibility for any errors or omissions. We specifically disclaim any liability resulting from the use or application of the information contained in this book.

To ensure compliance with requirements imposed by the IRS, we inform you that any US federal tax advice contained in this communication (including any attachments) is not intended or written to be used, and it cannot be used for the purpose of (i) avoiding penalties under the Internal Revenue Code or (ii) promoting, marketing, or recommending to another party any transaction or matter addressed herein. Always seek advice based on your particular circumstances from a qualified independent advisor.

Any disclosure, copying, or distribution of this material, or the taking of any action based on it, is strictly prohibited. All rights reserved. No part of this publication may be reproduced, stored in a retrieval system, or transmitted in any form or by any means, electronic, mechanical, photocopied, recorded, or otherwise, except in the case of brief quotations embodied in critical articles or reviews, without the prior written permission of the publisher. For more information, write US TaxAid Series, PO Box 158, Sparks, NV 89432.

Introduction

I remember huddling around the teletype machine, a giant noisy dot matrix, just before Christmas 1985. The new tax bill was coming and it was going to be earth shattering.

As it came off the printer, the tax manager at the CPA firm divided up sections and handed them off to the tax specialists at the big firm. I got trusts which didn't have a lot of big changes. The assigned S Corporation group moaned. It called for a dramatic change from the way we were used to planning for taxes.

A few partners decided to not learn the new tax law and instead opted for a lesser role in the firm. They were ready to retire.

We survived the 1986 Tax Reform Act. We'll survive the Tax Cuts and Jobs Act also known as the Trump Tax Plan. Already, there are loopholes galore for people who are willing to do a few things differently than they have in the past.

Taxmageddon 2018 looks at the massive tax changes that have occurred with the new Tax Act. But it's more than just deciphering the changes, you'll learn 95 strategies you can put in place right now to prepare you for less taxes and more control.

Let me be really clear.

The new Tax Act is a change. It's not the end. In fact, a lot of people are calling this change Armaggedon. You know, like the end. But it's not really. It's Taxmageddon, the end of one system and the beginning of another.

What Will Taxmageddon Mean for You?

A lot will depend on when you're reading this. If you are one of those who jump in early, ready to embrace the changes, you're likely to have a great result. If you're reading this a year after the Tax Cuts and Jobs Act went into effect, then you've probably already seen that tax planning isn't like it used to be. It's not the end. It's just a change.

Just imagine. Once you have the tools to understand exactly what Taxmageddon will mean for you in your current situation, you can determine when and how much you'll pay in taxes.

Will you have to do something differently? Sure. Nothing ever changes unless you first change what you do. And that all starts with changing how you view taxes.

All it takes is one change to make a big difference in the tax you pay. Imagine what you could do with the money you save. Invest it. Build a business. Change the future for your family and your community.

It all starts with change. And this book can help you create a roadmap for your change.

One more thing, don't forget to register your book. You will find the information you need to do that in. Once you've registered your book, you'll be able to join our private forum to discuss the hot new strategies with the new Tax Cuts and Jobs Act.

Stay current on hot new strategies! Information in Chapter 16!

Section I: Tax Act Strategies for Your Personal Return

Chapter 1: The Standard Deduction Vs Itemizing

It used to be that there was a wide variety of things you could deduct on your personal returns. I've been around in this field so long that I actually remember deducting credit card interest and car loan interest as itemized deductions on personal returns. There were lots of tax shelters that high income individuals could use to pay much less in taxes. That was then. Most of those tax shelters are gone now.

And, if you don't know it yet, you're about to find out soon that everything just changed dramatically for most taxpayers. Most of what was left as itemized deductions is gone now as well. We're left with just medical expenses over 7.5% of your adjusted gross income; mortgage interest (provided it qualifies); state and local income taxes and property taxes up to total maximum of $10,000, and charitable donations.

That's it.

Now let's look at what remains in a little more detail.

Qualified Medical Expenses
Qualified medical expenses are allowed when they are over 7.5% of adjusted gross income for 2018 and 2019. In 2020, the qualified medical expense deductibility threshold increases to 10% of your adjusted gross income.

There are two important income numbers you'll need to know for the Tax Cuts and Job Act. These are your adjusted gross income and your taxable income. These are not the same number. So please pay attention to that when you see something that talks about an income threshold. Is it your adjusted gross income or your taxable income or maybe even something different entirely that is being discussed?

When you determine how much of your medical expenses are deductible, you use the adjusted gross income number to determine the threshold. This is the bottom number on the first page of your Form 1040, Individual Tax Return. It's calculated as your total income minus some allowed adjustments. Tax forms in the future may change somewhat. But for as long as I can remember your adjusted gross income is at the bottom of the first page. It's also labeled on the form.

Remember the phrase "qualified medical expenses." Some expenses are allowed as deductions. Some are not.

A common question I'm asked is, "What's deductible?"

The IRS has some rules that don't always make sense, so at the risk of taking up a few pages of the book for this, let's look at what they say is now deductible and what is not. The deductible items are referred to as qualified medical expenses.

First, here's what is deductible.
- Acupuncture
- Air conditioner necessary for relief from allergies or other respiratory problems (less any increase in the value of your home resulting from installation of air conditioning)
- Alcoholism treatment, including inpatient treatment, meals and lodging at a therapeutic center for alcohol addiction
- Artificial limbs
- Artificial teeth
- Braille books and magazines used by a visually-impaired person
- A clarinet and lessons to treat the improper alignment of a child's upper and lower teeth
- Contact lenses, including equipment and materials for using contacts
- Cosmetic surgery, if it's necessary to improve a deformity related to a congenital abnormality, accident or disease
- Diet, special. When prescribed by a doctor, you can deduct the extra cost of purchasing special food to alleviate a specific medical condition
- Doctor or physician expenses

- Drug addiction treatment, including in-patient treatment, meals and lodging at a therapeutic center for drug addiction
- Elastic hosiery to treat blood circulation problems
- Exercise program if a doctor has recommended it as treatment for a specific condition
- Extra rent or utilities for a larger apartment required in order to provide space for a nurse/attendant
- Eye surgery, such as Lasik or a similar procedure, when it is not for cosmetic purposes only
- Guide dog or other animal used by a visually-impaired, hearing-impaired or otherwise physically disabled person
- Hospital care
- Household help for nursing care services only
- Insurance premiums for medical care coverage
- Laboratory fees
- Lead-based paint removal, including the cost of removing lead-based paints from surfaces when a child has lead poisoning or was previously diagnosed with lead poisoning. (Does not include the cost of repainting.)
- Legal fees paid to authorize treatment for mental illness
- Lifetime care advance payments
- Lodging expenses while away from home to receive medical care in a hospital or medical facility
- Long-term care insurance and long-term care expenses (there are limitations to what you can deduct)
- Mattresses and boards bought specifically to alleviate an arthritic condition
- Medical aids, including wheelchairs, hearing aids and batteries, eyeglasses, contact lenses, crutches, braces and guide dogs (and their care)
- Medical conference admission costs and travel expenses for a chronically ill person or a parent of a chronically ill child to learn about new medical treatments. (But not the cost of meals and lodging while attending the conference)
- Medicines and drugs
- Nursing care
- Nursing home expenses, including the entire cost of medical

- care, plus meals and lodging if the main reason for being in the home is to obtain medical care
- Oxygen and oxygen equipment
- Reclining chair bought on a doctor's advice by a person with a cardiac condition
- Special education; tuition for sending a mentally impaired or physically disabled person to a special school that has resources to relieve the disability
- Smoking cessation programs (does not have to be recommended by a physician)
- Swimming (the cost of therapeutic swimming prescribed by a physician)
- Telephone (the cost and repair of special telephone equipment for a hearing-impaired person)
- Television (the cost of equipment used to display the audio part of a TV program for hearing-impaired persons)
- Transplant of an organ (but not hair transplants)
- Transportation costs for obtaining medical care
- Travel expenses for parents visiting their child in a special school for children with drug problems, where the visits are part of the medical treatment
- Weight loss program, if it is recommended by a doctor to treat a specific medical condition or to cure any specific ailment or disease
- Whirlpool baths prescribed by a doctor
- Wig for the mental health of a patient who has lost his or her hair due to a disease, and
- X-ray services

Now, let's look at a few common medical expenses that aren't deductible.

- Antiperspirant
- Blemish concealer
- Chapstick/lip balm
- Cosmetic
- Dental floss

- Deodorant
- Drugs imported from other countries
- Dust masks
- Ensure
- Face creams
- Feminine hygiene products
- Hand/skin lotion
- Make-up
- Moisturizers
- Mouthwash
- Orajel Toothpaste
- Shampoo
- Shaving cream
- Soap
- Special foods
- Swabs
- Teeth whitening products
- Toothpaste/toothbrushes

Standard Deduction Increase

The standard deduction, which you can use instead of the itemized deduction, has greatly increased for tax years 2018 through 2025. The decrease in what you can itemize, coupled with the increase in the standard deduction, means a lot more people are going to skip itemization.

The standard deduction for 2018 through 2025 is $24,000 for married taxpayers, filing jointly, $12,000 for single filers and $16,000 for head of household filers.

Throughout *Taxmageddon 2018*, you will see suggested strategies. Some of them are strictly for use with your personal tax return. Other strategies are better suited to real estate investors and still others for business owners.

This first strategy in the book has to do with circumnavigating the massive change for individual tax returns.

Strategy # 1: Oscillating Deductions. *One of the most fundamental changes for individuals is the lessened benefit of itemizing your deductions. For years, we've been told to buy a bigger house, look for job-related expenses, write off alimony and even get a home equity loan. It didn't matter what the cost was; it was all tax deductible!*

Most of that stopped January 1, 2018. Itemized deductions have been stripped down to just medical expenses over 7.5% of your adjusted gross income, charitable contributions, mortgage interest on your qualifying residences (provided the total acquisition indebtedness is under $750,000), and state and local income tax and property tax. The total for the deduction for taxes is a maximum of $10,000 in total.

And, at the same time that less of your expenses are deductible, the amount of standard deductions has been increased to $12,000/$16,000/$24,000 (single/head of household/married, filing jointly). It's estimated that 80% of Americans will now file using only the standard deduction.

If you don't itemize, the deductions for mortgage interest, property tax, state tax and charity just don't matter. Buying a bigger house won't reduce your taxes. You quite likely lost at least some of the property tax and mortgage interest write-off for
your vacation home.

Now what?

If you're close to the breakeven of standard deduction/itemized deduction calculation, one strategy can be to stack up your itemized deductions every other year. For the most part, you can't control your state income tax or your medical expenses. You have much more control as to when you pay your property taxes or make charitable donations.

One strategy is to oscillate between itemized deductions and standard deductions. During the year that you plan to report the standard deduction versus itemized deductions, don't pay any more of your real property taxes than you need to. Hold off on your charitable donations. During the year that you plan to report itemized deductions, pay your property taxes for the year and make the beginning payment for the next year. Don't push any taxes until the next year. Double up on your charitable donations to make up for the year you missed.

If your medical expenses are exceeding the adjusted gross income threshold for one year and it's the year you're going to itemize, try to draw in as many medical expenses for that year as possible. If you have an expense that is going to be in December or January and December is the year you're itemizing and have a lot of medical expenses, pull the expense into December.

The idea is that you can maximize your total deductions by stacking up as many as possible for two years into the year you itemize and utilize the standard deductions in the off years.

If you live in a high-priced real estate area, you may have a hard time keeping your mortgage debt under the qualifying mortgage debt. For example, a starter home in some areas of southern California can be $1,000,000 or more. If you put down a lower down payment amount such as 10%, you'd have $900,000 of debt. Since the acquisition indebtedness limit is $750,000 for properties bought after January 1, 2018, you're only going to be able to take a deduction for part of the interest.

Strategy #2: Know Your Limits! *If your qualifying personal residence(s) were acquired prior to December 31, 2017, the allowable qualifying mortgage debt is $1,000,000 in total. If you purchased after that date, the allowable qualifying*
mortgage debt is reduced to $750,000.

If you have a vacation home, the interest may be deductible but only if the total debt for the vacation home and your primary residence are under the limits of $1,000,000 or $750,000.

This strategy is simply to know how much your debt is and have a strategy before you buy.

Personal Exemptions Are Gone
A common question we get at US Tax Aid Services, is whether someone can "claim" a child or an adult relative that the taxpayer helps support.

Sometimes people end up getting squeezed, supporting both their children and their parents and there is a sense of relief that at least you can get some kind of tax reduction by "claiming" them.
No more. The personal exemptions are gone.

It is possible to get a child tax credit is some cases. This has been increased to $2,000 per child under the age of 17 whom you are allowed to claim. If your child is older and in school or is older and disabled, you get a child tax credit of $500. The same is true for elderly relatives that live with you and that you support. You may get a tax credit of $500.

Remember that a tax credit is better than a tax deduction because the tax credit directly reduces the amount of tax you pay, while the deduction reduces the amount of taxable income you have, on which the tax is calculated.

Strategy #3: Dependent Exemption Replacement Strategy.
Starting in 2018, there are no longer any exemptions available for your dependents. One strategy may be to make your dependent a legitimate employee of your business. If you can pay your child, for example, you'll get a deduction from your personal income taxes and move income to his or her much lower tax rate.

Your child can then pay for his or her own non-deductible expenses such as college tuition and living expenses.

A Better Answer for the Lost Exemption Deduction
One of my clients has a profitable business and a high income. But, her money goes largely to support her elderly mother and her adult child.

Under the new tax law, there is a new possibility for her beyond the minimal $500 tax credits available for her mother and child. In reality, she wouldn't even get those because the credits phase out as income increases.

Because my client is single, there are two options for filing status: single and head of household. The head of household filing status will give her better tax brackets (and lower tax rates) and a bigger standard deduction. The standard deduction will change from $12,000 to $16,000.

In the past, the head of household filing status was determined by the people for which you get a dependency exemption. That's gone. So now what? Although at this moment, we don't have the definitive answer from the IRS, the old rule was that if there is someone you COULD claim a dependency exemption on but for some reason do not, you can claim head of household status.

That means supporting her mother will allow her to get the much-coveted head of household status. And that means a bigger deduction and less tax. The $500 tax credit won't matter because her income will phase it out.

Now what about her daughter who is out of high school and attends a few college classes, but isn't really interested in a college education?

We brainstormed some ways that her daughter could work in the taxpayer's business. In fact, my client had already made an offer to her daughter. Perfect! That meant she had a legitimate job handling some of the Internet aspects of the business. She would receive a salary that was deductible for my client. And because the daughter now had earned income, she could pick up more of her own expenses plus she wouldn't pay tax because she also received the much higher standard deduction. In fact, she won't pay tax until her income reaches $12,000. She can earn even more than that and not pay taxes if she decides to fund an IRA. Anything over that, and she would be taxed at a much lower tax rate, which is a big savings over her mother's tax rate.

Now that her child is an employee, there are additional perks that the business can give her, such as a car. It will be partially deductible by the business which is certainly better than the taxpayer paying for a car with after tax income and no deduction. She can put her adult child on the business medical insurance plan. If the adult child takes a class that can be helpful to her business job, the cost of the class, books and supplies will also be deductible for the business.

Bottom line: After the new Tax Act, the strategies are different! If you have a child who works in your business, or could work in your business, hire him or her. You get the deduction in your business for the salary you pay and they get to offset the income with the big standard deduction and take advantage of lower tax rate tables.

Strategy #4: Older Dependent Strategy. *If you have an older dependent that you support, you also just lost a dependency exemption for him or her. One idea might be to make your elderly relative a Director of your company. That way you can provide tax-free benefits like the medical expense reimbursement plan (MERP).*

Just like when you hire a dependent for your business as an employee, a Director position has to be legitimate. It has to be reasonable that you would have your relative in that position and that they provide legitimate value for the business.

Remember that if you add a nondiscriminatory plan like a MERP, you can't discriminate. Other full-time employees need to receive the same benefits. Talk to your tax advisor before you add such a plan.

Mortgage Interest is Limited

The previous tax law allowed you to take an interest deduction for a mortgage of up to $1,000,000 for qualified residence acquisition debt.

Let's unpack that statement.

First of all, note that the statement says "qualified residence." That doesn't mean just the primary residence. It means primary and, if applicable, a qualified vacation home, but only to a maximum combined total of $1,000,000 of debt.

That statement still needs a little further explanation. Acquisition indebtedness refers to the debt you used to buy your property. If you later do a cash-out refinance to pull money out with a larger loan, interest payments on the extra debt is not deductible. You can't go higher than your acquisition indebtedness with a new loan and keep the deduction.

Starting with purchases in 2018, your maximum allowed qualified residence acquisition indebtedness is $750,000.

Deductions for Home Equity Loans
The Trump Tax Plan initially seemed to indicate that you would lose the interest for home equity loans. The IRS subsequently issued a statement that stated you could still keep the interest as a deduction provided the total of the mortgage and the home equity loan (HELOC) were less than the old limit of $1,000,000 or the new limit of $750,000. The difference applies to when you bought the property. If you have a home equity loan in place and it had a balance at December 31, 2017, the old limit applies.

The IRS stressed that the HELOC proceeds must be used to improve or maintain your qualifying residence. Period.

One question that came out early when the Tax Act passed was how to handle a Home Equity Line of Credit that was in place as of December 31, 2017 but had no debt. Could you still borrow against it and take the interest as a deduction using the old limits? We're still waiting to see what the final IRS decision is on this one.

Strategy #5: When You Take a Questionable Position. Now is a good time to talk about this compliance strategy. Since we don't know absolutely how the IRS will treat a HELOC deduction for a property pre-2018, but without a loan in place, you may want to take a more aggressive position.

If you take a position on your tax return that isn't clear-cut, make sure you disclose the position in a statement on your return. That way you have given proper notice to the IRS and if there is later a problem, they can't hit you with excessive penalties.

And, let's talk about one more way to deduct your interest. This works when other ways might not.

Strategy #6: Save Your Home Equity Interest! You can save your Home Equity interest deduction or cash-out refinance loan deduction by proving the extra money was used for your business or real estate. Provide good records showing that the amount borrowed was deposited into the applicable business or real estate accounts. Also, draw up a note with the business and real estate business entities. This shows that you clearly had the intent to take a loan for your business or real estate and that you did use the money for business and/or real estate.

State and Local Taxes are Limited

Single, head of household and married, filing jointly taxpayers can deduct up to $10,000 of state and local taxes. This limitation includes your property tax. If you're married, filing separately, you can only deduct up to $5,000.

Charitable Contribution Deductions Are Expanded

The Tax Cuts and Job Act increases the cash contribution limit from 50% to 60% of your adjusted gross income. However, you do need to itemize deductions in order to take the charitable contribution deduction.

__Strategy #7: Save Your Charitable Donations__. Is the small charity dead? It's estimated that 80% or more of all Americans will no longer file with itemized deductions. They'll all use the standard deduction. That means smaller donors likely won't care about the deduction, or at least that will be true when it sinks in that everything has changed. Existing 501 (c) (3) charities will likely stay with a non-profit status, at least for a while. But the cost and hassle of maintenance may eventually be more than the benefits. This doesn't mean that charitable causes will go away. It simply means that it may become unnecessary for them to go through the cost and hassle of getting non-profit status.

If you have a small charity, or care about supporting one, find ways to make sure your donors have something other than the tax deductions that keeps them engaged and active in your cause! If you have a small charity, you may decide to stop the reporting hassle and cost of remaining a 501 (c) (3) because it won't help your donors. Time will tell how this change will impact the charities. For now, just be aware.

Charities continue to be a good tax savings strategy for higher income taxpayers who are charitably minded. In fact, the previous limit of 50% of adjusted gross income for current charitable donations has been increased to 60% of adjusted gross income for the deduction. It's better than ever in the right set of circumstances!

Strategy #8: High Income Charitable Cause. *Create your own 501 (c)(3) to support your charitable passion while building a future for yourself.*

A new client with a very high paying job in the tech industry was looking for a way out.

"What do you want to do?", I asked.

She was buying up real estate to provide passive cash flow when she left her job. But it seemed like her heart wasn't really into it. I understand that. Real estate can be a great way to provide passive income, appreciation and tax breaks, but not everyone loves it.

She thought for a second and then blurted out, "I want to help the homeless problem in the US."

She then went on to tell me about the details for a master plan to provide shelter and counseling for some of the most disenfranchised people in our society. It was a workable plan and it was clear she had a lot of passion.

And, it was something that could give her a tax break right now. Normally, we talk about the tax breaks for real estate but because she had another job and her income was high, she couldn't take advantage of the paper losses from real estate.

Charitable donations, though. That was something that she could deduct.

She set up her own non-profit with the 501 (c) (3) designation and began funding it with deductible donations. Some of the money went to existing programs. Some of it was saved up for some bigger projects.

All of the donations were deductible.

At some point, she plans to quit her tech job and go to work for her charity. At that point, her income will be much lower and she plans to live on $50,000 or less per year. It'll be taxable income for her, but the tax she pays at the lower tax rate *will be much lower than the tax rate benefit she got for the donation made when her income was higher.*

In a way, it's like paying for a future annuity. In this case, she's building toward her dreams of helping others.

Miscellaneous Itemized Deductions

All miscellaneous itemized deductions have been repealed until 2025.

In the next few chapters, we're going to explore new tax-saving strategies for otherwise lost itemized deductions and dependent deductions.

Chapter 2: The Loss of Miscellaneous Deductions

Effective January 1, 2018, miscellaneous itemized deductions are gone until 2025. These lost deductions include the following items.

Alimony
For any divorce or separation agreement after December 31, 2018, alimony payments pursuant to those agreements will not be deductible by the spouse who pays. Also the spouse who receives the payment will not need to report the alimony as taxable income.

If you have a divorce or separation agreement prior to that date, the alimony payments continue to be deductible.

Strategy #9: Alimony Change*. This is a strategy that every good divorce attorney already knows. The negotiations just got a whole lot more interesting. In the past, alimony was more willingly paid because it was deductible by the wealthier spouse. Child support was not deductible. So, occasionally, the trade-off was made for less child support and higher alimony. The tax deduction helped.*

Since additional property transfers don't have any tax consequence, likely alimony payments will be less now that they aren't a deductible expense to the payer and property transfers will be greater.

The only viable strategy here is to consider all options and "crunch the numbers." What is the real cost of alimony paid if you lose the tax deduction?

Remember that for agreements signed prior to December 31, 2018, the old law will remain. I suspect we'll see a very busy fall and winter 2018 for most divorce attorneys.

Moving Expenses
The moving expense deduction is repealed through 2025. There is an exception for military on active duty who move due to a military order. Those costs will still be at least partially deductible.

Strategy #10: Tax-Deductible Move. Your business can make a tax deductible move. However, the new law does state that if an employee (or owner) of a business moves, the cost to move personal items is not deductible. Your business also can't reimburse you for personal moving costs.

The strategy here would be to include as many items in the business side of the move as reasonably possible. For example, the furniture in your home office would be covered by a deductible moving expense. The cost to move kitchen items probably would not be a deductible expense.

You can't pick up all of your moving expenses with this strategy, but at least some is better than nothing.

Bicycle Commuting Reimbursement.
This deduction for employees is gone through 2025.

Strategy #11: Write Off Bicycles. Do you have a company that is somehow involved in bicycles? Or, do you work for a company that does? Maybe you sell them, repair them, tour with them, paint them or have affiliate links to sales, repairs, tours or decoration. If so, you may need to have bicycles as part of the promotion and marketing of your company. You win! You still have a bicycle deduction. Otherwise, the bicycle commuting deduction is gone.

Unreimbursed Job Expenses

Another miscellaneous itemized deduction was unreimbursed job expenses. This was a deduction that was used by people who paid union dues, had to buy, clean and pay for the repair of uniforms or in the case of people who traveled and weren't reimbursed by their employer for the cost of travel, auto expense and meals. Generally, the taxpayer is a W-2 employee who is responsible for costs incurred while doing his or her job.

And now, effective in 2018, it's no longer a miscellaneous itemized deduction.

Strategy #12: Employee or Independent Contractor? If you can change your W-2 job into an independent contractor (IC) position you may be able to pick up some of those lost itemized deductions. For example, the unreimbursed job expense is no longer a deduction for employees. It would be a *deduction for an Independent Contractor. Talk to your employer!*

The IC status can be a tricky area for employer/contractors, especially if the worker was formerly an employee. The IRS would want to see that something substantial has changed that warrants a change in status from employee to IC. Remember, the IRS would rather keep you reporting as an employee. That means more taxes.

Another idea is that perhaps you can negotiate a fixed payment amount for these extra costs that is covered by your employer in lieu of part of your salary. You'll get less income, but, in reality, you end up putting more in your pocket because the extra items that are paid for by your employer don't have payroll or federal and state income tax assessed. Plus, your employer should be happier because they won't have to pay payroll taxes on that portion of payment. It's a reimbursement, not a salary.

Tax Preparation

Tax preparation is another expense you won't be able to deduct starting in 2018. It may not be as big a deal as some of the other items, but I'm a CPA, so I'll be a little biased. I think it's an important expense.

Strategy #13: Tax Prep Deduction. *Have your accountant send you a separate bill to break out your business and real estate investment accounting from the tax preparation costs. The business part will continue to be deductible against business income. Your real estate expenses will be a deduction against real estate income. It's just the purely personal tax preparation part that won't be deductible.*

Theft or Casualty Loss

The theft loss deduction and the casualty loss deduction, except from a federally designated disaster zone, go away. Unless these losses happen to you, you may not realize how important this deduction really was.

Suppose someone breaks in and steals from you. That's a theft loss and not only does it feel personal and violating, it can be a significant financial loss as well.

Something similar happened in my family. My elderly mother had a trusted caregiver who stole almost $100,000, valuable personal property and my mother's late model car (which was later found stripped out.) There is no chance for recovery, so I was grateful for the write-offs for her 2016 and 2017 returns. (The timing was based on when we discovered the items were gone and the knowledge was certain that there was little to no recovery.) That sort of tax relief is gone!

If the losses had occurred one or two years later, there would have been no deduction. Since the total loss was almost $200,000, that was a significant issue.

Strategy #14: Theft Loss Timing. *If you have a theft loss in which the discovery is still ongoing, it may be hard to pinpoint exactly when it has occurred. If there is a way to try to pull some of those theft losses into 2017, it will be deductible as a miscellaneous itemized deduction. In 2018 and later years, it will not be.*

Timing on an Investment Fraud
Just before the end of 2017, I had a consultation with a new client. As we sorted through the various issues, I spotted that they had possibly lost a little under $200,000 in an investment. Based on the initial notes, the promoter and others had criminal charges pending against them. The money, as far as anyone could tell, was gone.

In any other year, I might have waited until 2018 to see how the case developed, but this year, we needed to move quickly to capture the loss in 2017. There will be a big write-off in 2017 but if we had waited there would be none in 2018.

The issue is "timing." When can the loss be taken? It's not whether there is a loss. That's pretty certain. The question is when is it a legally deductible loss?

The Tax Court has dealt with several cases resembling this. You must have reasonable certainty you won't recoup your money. You aren't required to have "incorrigible optimism." If there is only a remote chance that you will recover, you probably would have a write-off in 2017 but not in 2018.

Additionally, you need to be able to show you have credible evidence. You have to show that you really had a loss and demonstrate what that financial amount will be.

The best solution, the one we'll be using, is to include a statement by an independent third party as to the amount of the loss and the slim chance of any amount of recovery. That will be attached to the taxpayer's tax return to provide proof.

If later there is recovery, that amount will need to be added to the personal income for that year.

This case won't be applicable for everyone, but for those for whom it fits, it can be very valuable. Talk to your experienced CPA.

Strategy #14: Business Theft Losses. *Business theft losses will still be deductible as a business expense. If you have a theft personally, it's not deductible. If you have a theft in your business, it's deductible. Carefully consider where the loss actually occurs. If it is a business loss, it's a deduction.*

Individual Alternative Minimum Tax (AMT)
Sadly, AMT is still around for individuals. The phase-out thresholds may have been raised, but there are still bound to be some people surprised.

AMT is not widely understood by most taxpayers. Even when you carefully do tax planning, you may sometimes find out later that you owe thousands of dollars due to AMT. The concept is too strange for most people to truly master.

That's because AMT is a shadow tax system that isn't discussed or even planned, for in most cases.

Here's how it works. You start with your regular taxable income. This is the income that is shown in the top 1/3 of page 2 of your Form 1040. It's your adjusted gross income from the bottom of page one, less your standard deduction or itemized deductions and exemptions (which go away in 2018). Certain tax preference items must be recalculated and added back to your regularly calculated taxable income to find your AMT taxable income.

For example, you know that tax-exempt interest you received? It's not exempt for AMT purposes. It is added back into income. Your depreciation is re-calculated. Other expenses are not allowed. Capital gains is taxed at a higher percentage than what you expect and definitely higher than you report on your "normal" tax return. And, perhaps the biggest shock of all for people who have big net operating loss (NOL) carryovers, the NOL deduction is not allowed to offset AMT income.

When the new calculation is made, the AMT tax rate is applied to the AMT calculated income. If you had a lot of tax preference items that gave you great tax breaks for regular taxable income, you might be surprised to find you suddenly owe more tax!

There was a lot of talk that AMT would go away with the Tax Act. Sadly, even though it did go away for C Corporations, it is still around for individuals.

Strategy #16: AMT Strategy. *When it comes to AMT, it's important to HAVE an AMT strategy. One of your year-end tax planning strategy questions should be to ask if you have a possibility of an AMT issue. This is a question for a qualified tax preparer. Unless you have a professional tax software program and are educated and experienced in the tax field, specifically with AMT, do not try to do this at home.*

If the answer is "yes" when you ask if you should be worrying about AMT, your next question is "How do I plan for this?"

Sometimes you may want to accelerate or delay deductions that are going to be wiped out with the AMT calculation. If there is one event that is triggering it for the current year, put off deductions that you're going to lose anyway.

The biggest strategy for dealing with AMT is to pay attention. Do not ignore it. Plan for it. If it's an issue for you in the current tax year, then you actually need two strategies: one for regular tax and one for AMT.

Net Operating Loss
First of all, I want to clarify that net operating losses occur with businesses. Sometimes NOL gets confused with the real estate suspended losses.

In the case of real estate, if you have passive real estate losses, those may need to be suspended. If your adjusted gross income is under $100,000, you can deduct up to $25,000 of real estate passive losses. If your adjusted gross income is over $150,000, you are not allowed to deduct any losses. Between $100,000 and $150,000, the amount you can deduct is phased out. Unless you are a real estate professional in the eyes of the IRS, the rest of any real estate loss is suspended. Now, after that rather long explanation, I want to clarify.

Suspended passive real estate losses are not NOL.

Net operating loss is a business loss that either came from a Schedule C Sole proprietorship or through one of your pass-through business entities. In the past, you had a choice of first taking the loss backwards to wipe out high income years and then, if there was additional loss, carrying it forward. Now, in 2018, you can only carry losses forward.

If you currently have NOL carrying forward, you can continue to do so under the old rules. For new NOL, you can only use the NOL to offset up to 80% of your total income.

In other words, even if you have a huge loss that is carrying forward, you still have to pay some tax.

Too Many Losses
I like to do a lot of preparation before consultations with new clients. When you have a consultation with me you'll get asked a lot of questions about the businesses you have now, what businesses you plan to start, what your income currently is and what you project it will be. I'll ask you to tell me about your dreams and your goals. And about your challenges with those businesses and investments. Then finally I'll ask you how I can best help you.

A new client was concerned that he had a lot of carryforward NOL that wasn't being used. His main questions all revolved about how to use those losses. He'd read what I, and others, had said about NOL and he wanted to know why he wasn't getting the deduction.

"That seems strange," I thought. NOLs are deductible against income.

As I looked at his last tax return, I spotted a few things that I wanted to investigate. Before we even had our consultation, I asked for more information and in this case, it meant more years' worth of tax returns.

The answer was in the past tax returns.

My new client actually had several carryforward losses on his return. He also had some suspended real estate losses. That likely wasn't going to change, but we wanted to stop the bleeding, so I recommended he stop taking depreciation. Depreciation is a strange type of deduction. You can take it, or not. You can catch it up. You can accelerate it with a cost segregation study. And you can just stop it, after you've already started it.

Since depreciation has to be recaptured when you sell and he received no benefit from the additional loss it created, he, in effect, was exchanging capital gains tax (maximum of 20%) for depreciation recapture tax (25%). Not a smart strategy.

He also had capital loss carryforward. In case of this type of carryforward, your deduction is limited to the amount of capital gains in that year plus $3,000. Sometimes I see clients with losses of $100,000 or more. Recently, a new client showed a loss of $300,000. It would take 100 years to get the full tax benefit of that loss. He needed a whole different strategy.

In the case of my consulting client, he needed to turn ordinary income into capital gains income. Not hard, if you have enough time to plan and are willing to do things a little differently. (For more details on this strategy, please go to Chapter 16 to register your book and refer to *Insider Tax Strategies*, a free bonus as a thank you for your purchase of *Taxmageddon 2018*.)

And then we got to the net operating loss. He was absolutely right. He had net operating losses that were carried forward and he was not using those losses to offset his other income.

In this case, the issue was that he did not have sufficient basis. There are actually two requirements that must be met before net operating losses can even be considered to offset other income. These are:

1. You need to have active participation in the business, and
2. You need to have basis.

Active participation is a pretty low standard, as tax rules go. It means you have to be active in the business. For example, if you go over the financials with the CFO and talk to the manager a few times a week as a way to stay in touch and help focus on what the company can do better, you have active participation!

Basis, though, is a little trickier. There are two types of basis that qualify. One is equity basis. Equity is comprised of the money you put in the company that isn't just a loan. If you make a loan, it's not equity, it's a liability for the company. The loan will increase your debt basis, but not your equity basis.

If you fund your company with $10,000, you have $10,000 in equity. Over time, there is income the company will make. Your share of the income increases your basis. If there is company loss, your share of the loss decreases your basis. If you take out a distribution, it decreases your basis as well.

If the business has a flow-through loss to you, you need to tally up the equity basis you have. If you don't have enough equity basis, you may not be able to take a deduction for the loss.

You do have one more shot, though. You may have enough debt basis. If you have loaned your business money, that adds to the debt basis. In the case of a partnership, or an LLC that has elected to be taxed as a partnership, if you have personally guaranteed partnership debt then it will count as well.

However, in the case of an S Corporation or an LLC that elects to be taxed as an S Corporation, if you personally guarantee the debt, that will not count toward the debt basis.

That's an important difference to keep in mind.

In this case, my new client didn't have enough basis. He had a lot of debt, but he had not personally contributed the money and because it was an S Corporation, the fact that he had personally guaranteed the debt didn't count.

Over the next year, the company paid off that debt and he personally loaned money to the corporation so that he had the needed debt basis.

The corporation didn't have enough cash to pay off the debt without getting a loan. This time, though, they got the loan through the owner so he could get basis. That meant he could take advantage of the net operating losses he had carried over.

The lesson to take away from this real-life story is to first understand what kind of carryforward loss you have and then figure out what needs to change in order for you to use that loss to offset other income.

Strategy #17: Check Your Basis. *In reality, the only way you won't have enough basis is if you've received loans from outside parties or if your business has received deposits for work that it has not yet done or earned. In some cases, loans from outside parties that you personally guarantee can be used to increase your basis.*

If you are operating through a partnership, you get basis if you personally guarantee the loan. If you are operating through an S Corporation, guaranteeing a loan does not give you personal basis.

The Importance of Strategy

Throughout this book, we'll talk a lot about strategy. A strategy actually comes in the middle. First, you need a good assessment of where you are and then clear goals of where you want to be. What do you want to accomplish? What are you willing to do to get there? I don't mean rob a bank or cause someone harm, but are you willing, for example, to start a business? To form a different business structure? To move?

Once you know where you are going, where you want to be and the absolutes of what you will and will not do, then look at what strategies will work best for you.

You're still not done yet! You have to implement the strategies. Most likely you will need the help of some legal and tax specialists to do that. You could have the best strategy in the world, but, if implemented incorrectly, it could be very costly to you.

And then, finally, you need to report it correctly. If you don't follow the very specific reporting requirements, you may have big problems from the IRS or your state taxing authority later on.

Chapter 3: Strategies for Your Personal Residence

The Trump Tax Plan has some notable changes when it comes to deductions for your personal residence and vacation residence. There could have been more changes but at the last minute, Congress cut us a break.

For example, at one point, the personal residence capital gains exclusion was proposed to be changed. In the end, it was not changed. It's the same rule. If you live in your home for 2 of the previous 5 years and then sell it for a gain, part of that gain will not be subject to capital gains tax. If you're married, filing jointly, you can exclude up to $500,000 of capital gains. If you're single, you can exclude up to $250,000 of gain. That all stayed the same. The rules still require that you need to have lived in the home 2 of the previous 5 years to take advantage of the capital gains exclusion.

Strategy #18: Fix & Move Every Two Years. *This strategy is one that I've talked about for years. I have clients who love the challenge of a fixer upper and as their CPA, I love the strategy that lets them make income tax-free.*

In this case, they buy properties that are undervalued and usually the worst house in a good neighborhood. They move in and fix it up. Wait a total of 2 years and then sell. Since they're married, they can take a capital gains exclusion of up to $500,000 on the sale of the home.

Generally, they make $100,000 or so, not $500,000 once you calculate all of the improvement costs. But remember that is tax free money. And they've lived in the house during that whole time. No rental expenses.

If you have a flair for decorating or love to fix things, this could work for you! I've seen clients turn big homes into turn-key assisted living centers or rehab centers. They sell the house as their personal residence, but with a plan and all set up to change the function of the space into a money maker. What can you do to make a home even more valuable? Remember you've got a big chunk of money coming to you tax free!

I frequently am asked how the gain is calculated when you sell your home. It doesn't matter how much the loan is or how much cash you receive when you sell. The calculation is based on basis (the amount you paid plus what you spent on improvements).

Sales Price
-Cost of Sales (commission, etc.)
-Basis
= Gain/Loss

If you had previously depreciated some or all of your home, you will need to recapture that depreciation. In that case, the formula becomes:

Sales Price
-Cost of Sales
-Basis
+Accumulated Depreciation
= Gain/Loss

The Accumulated Depreciation does not receive the same tax-free capital gains exclusion that the overall gain will.

Another strategy that takes advantage of the capital gains exclusion rule is to simply move into your rental properties. It's not quite as straight forward, though. In fact, Congress has put several limits on how much will be allowed to be covered with the capital gains exclusion. Here's how that works.

Moving into Your Rental Property
In the past, it's been an attractive strategy to chain together rental properties so that the owner(s) can move into one after the other every two years and never pay tax when they sell.

Congress and the IRS have passed several rules to limit the blanket capital gains exclusion in this case. One of these you may know. The other is rarely talked about, but can come back and bite you, if you're not careful!

First, the IRS stated that depreciation would still be subject to recapture. So, if you've had the rental property for any period of time, you've accrued accumulated depreciation that you pay tax on regardless. That part of the law has been around since 1997, so it shouldn't be as big of a surprise as the next part.

In the Housing Assistance Tax Act of 2008, Congress added another wrinkle to capital gains exclusion for property that had been converted from a rental to a primary residence prior to sale. The additional rule states that the capital gains exclusion is specifically available only for periods during which the property was actually used as a primary residence. This came into effect January 1, 2009, so if the property was only rented prior to that time, this new rule would not be applicable.

If the property was used first as a rental after January 1, 2009, this period of time is called "nonqualifying use." The gains are then allocated between nonqualifying use and qualifying use and the exclusion amount is pro-rated.

Rental Than Primary Residence
Let's say that you owned a property for 6 years. For the first 4 years you rented the property out. You then lived in the home as a primary residence for the next 2 years. You had a total of $150,000 of capital gains over the 6 year period.

However, you lived in the home for 2 out of 6 years since 2009, so only 1/3 (2 divided by 6) of the capital gains will be considered qualifying use. That means you have a capital gains exclusion of $50,000 (1/3 of $150,000). Of course, there is depreciation which also must be recaptured.

Strategy #19: Rental to Primary Strategy. If you move into a property that had been used as rental after 2009, the longer you live in the property as your primary residence, the better your ratio for write-offs. For example, if it was a rental for 2 years and then you lived in the property for 2 years, half of the gain will be subject to the capital gains exclusion. On the other hand, if it was a rental for 2 years and then you lived in it for 4 years, 2/3 of the gain would be subject to the capital gains exclusion (4 years divided by 6 years total).

Remember that this applies only for the years that were rented after January 1, 2009 and only if you rented the property first and then moved into it. If you had it as your primary residence first, and then rented it, the 2 out of 5 years rule will apply.

Moving into a Rental Property After a 1031 Exchange
One of the best tax deferral strategies for real estate is to exchange your appreciated property for another real estate property. You have to sell and buy your properties within 180 days, invest all of the cash you receive and your other property must be purchased for at least the amount of the sales price. You also need to not touch any of the cash from the sale and you must list out possible exchanged properties to purchase within 45 days. That's a very short synopsis of a 1031 exchange. Since it's not part of the Tax Cuts and Jobs Act, it's not included in this book. If you want more information about this unique strategy of delaying tax on the gain from the sale of your property, please go to Chapter 16 for information on how to register your book. You'll find more information there as well as a lively forum to answer your tax questions. This is available exclusively for *Taxmageddon 2018* readers.

The 1031 exchange (aka Starker exchange aka like-kind exchange) isn't tax free. It is a tax deferral. You roll over the gain until you sell the subsequent property or properties that you purchased. You then pay tax on the gain from the first sale and gain on the subsequent sale.

But, what if you could roll over an appreciated rental property into a home you want to move into? And then, later, after you've spent the requisite time in your new primary residence, take advantage of the capital gains exclusion on the sale.

Congress changed the rules in the case of a 1031 exchange that rolls to a primary residence. In this case you receive the capital gains exclusion on a primary residence if you lived in it for 5 years since the exchange. This is not the 2 out of 5 year exclusion. It's a different time period.

Let's look at an example. Let's say that you owned a commercial building since 2000 and then did a qualifying 1031 exchange to a single family home in 2011 with the intention of moving into the home. If you move into the home right away and live in it for 5 years, you have the full capital gains exclusion of $500,000 (married filing jointly) or $250,000 (single).

If you instead rent the house first for 2 years and then move in for 3 years, you've waited the required 5 years. But, you won't be able to get the full capital gains exclusion. You will have 3/5 of qualifying use, so receive 3/5 of capital gains exclusion amount.

All of the above changes have occurred prior to the Trump Tax Plan. The new changes didn't get a lot of press, so I find that a lot of my new clients don't realize that the rules have changed. That's why I've started off with those. Now, let's look at what specifically has changed for primary residence deductibility under the Tax Cuts and Jobs Act.

Changes for Primary Residences with the Tax Cuts and Jobs Act

At one point, we thought that vacation homes would not be included for the mortgage interest deduction and property tax deduction on Schedule A, Itemized Deductions. In the final version of the Act, we discovered that vacation homes are still considered qualified residences. However, there are limitations for the total that is allowed to be deducted.

We are left with three major changes for home owners.

1. Home Equity Loans deductibility is limited.
2. The deduction for Mortgage Interest is limited.
3. The deduction for Property Tax is limited.

Home Equity Loans Deductibility is Limited

A home equity loan is a loan that uses the equity in your home as collateral for a loan. One of the most common forms is a line of credit (LOC) or home equity line of credit (HELOC), which allows you to borrow against the equity as desired. You can carry any amount of balance, up to the terms of your lending agreement.

If you had an existing home equity loan at the end of December 31, 2017, the interest on this loan will continue to be deductible. If you have a new HELOC, you may be subject to the new reduced limit of $750,000 of acquisition indebtedness in total (primary mortgage plus HELOC) for qualifying residences (primary residence and possible vacation residence.)

In an earlier strategy, Strategy #6 in Chapter 1, we discussed a way to make the interest deductible by using the funds for your business or your real estate. It doesn't mean you report the interest as a Schedule A, Itemized Deduction as in the past. Instead the interest expense in this case will be deducted as a business or real estate expense.

The Mortgage Interest Deduction is Limited
Effective in 2018, the mortgage interest deduction is limited to the interest on up to $750,000 of acquisition indebtedness for qualifying property.

If you have a mortgage debt acquired prior to 2018, the old acquisition indebtedness limit of $1,000,000 still applies.

If you have a vacation property, the mortgage interest deduction and debt limitation applies to it as well in total. In other words, you have a total indebtedness allowed of $1,000,000. It's not $1,000,000 per property.

It should be mentioned that this restriction is only for the itemized deductions. If you have a rental property with a larger debt, the interest charge associated with that will still be deductible no matter how large the debt. You may have a paper loss, though, that is suspended and carried forward. That has to do with your own personal situation and whether your passive real estate losses are limited.

The Deduction for Property Tax is Limited
The sum of the deduction for property tax plus state and local tax has a cap of $10,000 per year. Period. This is going to be a problem for

individuals that itemize in high income tax and property tax states like California, New York and Illinois.

Now is the time to plan what your strategies are going to be!

Strategy #20: Rent the House You Live in. *This strategy might seem a little extreme, especially if you're firmly ensconced in your current home. In general, though, let's take a look at what the new tax law changes really mean. We've always heard that it's a smart financial and tax strategy to own your home. It'll go up in value, you won't be throwing money away on rent plus the government will let you take a tax deduction for interest on the loan to buy it.*

After 2008-2009, a lot of people realized that real estate has no guarantee that it will always go up in value. And now, your deductions will be limited for property tax and mortgage interest. You might just find the limited write-offs don't mean a thing to you since you will be better off using the higher standard deduction than itemizing your deductions.

So, what if instead of buying your own home, you bought a rental? Expenses associated with the rental are fully deductible. Even if your income means you can't immediately take a deduction, the loss is just suspended, not lost.

Another idea works if you can find someone who wants to live in a house that is similar to yours. Buy their house and they rent it from you. They buy your house and you rent it from them. You may even have options to repurchase each other's houses at a later date.

The main point out of all of this is that our view of our personal residence is changing. Owning your own personal home no longer provides the tax advantages that you're used to planning on.

High Living Rental
A very successful real estate investor client of mine has had one rule for years.

Rent where you live.

He buys primarily working class residential rentals, including single family homes all the way to 100+ apartment buildings. But he wants to live in luxury homes and he discovered early on that when you look at the COCR (cash on cash return), owning luxury rentals simply isn't attractive. If you own a luxury rental, you get a very low return on your investment. In fact, you usually are upside down. The payments are frequently larger than the rental payment you get. That's a bad investment if you're the owner, but great value if you're the renter.

Instead, he rents where he lives and uses the down-payment he would have needed to buy the luxury home for more investment properties that give him good cash flow.

Strategy #21: Rent Out Part of Your House. *If you rent part of your house, you can move part of the mortgage interest and property tax expense from itemized deductions, which are limited, to rental expenses.*

For example, if you rent out 50% of your house, then 50% of your mortgage interest and 50% of your property tax will be deductible.

If you also depreciate that part of your house, you will need to add back in that depreciation when you sell your house. When you sell, you may also have some capital gains tax to pay. Normally, if you live in your house for 2 of the previous 5 years, you will get a capital gains exclusion of $250,000 (single) or $500,000 (married filing jointly). But since you have converted 50% of the home to business use, you now have 50% of the gains that will be taxable. One possible strategy in this case is to kick out your tenant and live in the whole home long enough so that you can take advantage of the 2 out of 5 year exclusion.

It's clear that the way we view our home will change over the next few years. If the mortgage interest deduction is an issue for you, you could pay off your home loan. Of course, you probably won't be getting a very good return for your money. The biggest issue for most of my clients, though, will be the limitation on state and local taxes and property taxes.

If you aren't willing to change your lifestyle for taxes, and let's face it, not everyone wants to do that, you will lose some deductions. Less deductions means more tax, unless you find another way to replace the deductions you just lost. The next Section will have more ideas

you might use if so far you're under-impressed with your options in dealing
with the loss of itemized deductions.

Strategy #22: Downsize. *If you want more money, there are two ways to do that: Increase income and/or decrease expenses. The American Dream is to want a big home and as your income goes up, get a bigger home. While I'm far from the most frugal person, I do recognize the trap people get into when they get bigger and bigger houses.*

Unfortunately, the bigger house means more furniture, bigger property tax, more maintenance costs, higher insurance cost. You will probably find living in a bigger house means you will need more fashionable clothes, more expensive personal maintenance, more expensive work-outs, golf club dues, private schools and more. You think your expenses went up 50% because of the new house costs? Look again. I bet they went up a whole lot more.

What if instead of a bigger house, you got a smaller one? You would have more free cash for investments and not have your tax deduction limited.

More Income, Less Money

I recently had a client quit working with my firm. He didn't like the strategies we came up with. We found a few things initially that could have been reported differently, but it came down to the fact that he wanted dramatically different results and didn't want to make any changes.

Unfortunately, I see similar stories all too often. Typically, it's a high income household and the parents work long hours at jobs they really don't like. It could even be in a business that they own or a profession they've spent years training for such as a doctor. But the fact is that it has become a treadmill for them. And it's one that keeps going faster and faster. There needs to be some reward! And generally, that means spending money. Money for travel, money for luxuries such as sports cars, and money for a bigger house and all that goes with it.

In the end, the family that works very hard to make $300,000 - $500,000 per year, can have nothing left at the end of the month. The answer isn't always to make more money. Sometimes it's a question of making sure the money you spend is an investment, with ROI (return on investment) instead of just an expense. If you can't turn it into an investment, at least make sure you're maximizing your deductions.

But for people who don't want to change, it's hard for me to help them make a difference in the taxes they pay. Things have to change and there does have to be some money spent to set up entities, fund a pension, send money to a C Corporation for services or whatever is involved in their strategy. There is always a rate of return on our strategies, but it does take some money to implement it. And it will require some changes in how business is done. Sometimes those changes are too much for some people to make.

Strategy #23: Set up a home office. *In the next section, we'll talk about starting a business. In order to have a home office, you'll need to have a business. So, in a way, I have jumped the gun a little bit on this strategy. It is a powerful one, though, for your home and especially important now that we may be looking at losing part or all of the itemized deductions.*

In order to have a home office you first must have a business. You need to have a space that is regularly and exclusively used for that business. If you can meet those requirements, the next step is to determine your business use percentage. Measure your square footage of the office space and the total square footage of the house.

Divide the business office space by the total space and you will come up with the business percentage.

Now apply that percentage to your indirect costs such as mortgage interest, property tax, insurance, HOA dues, utilities, maintenance and the like. If there are expenses directly associated with the home office, those are 100% deducted.

The IRS also offers a simplified method to claim the home office. But, in most cases, the method above, with actual numbers, will give you a better deduction.

If you sell your home at a profit, you do not have to allocate any part of the gain to the business portion. In other words, you get a deduction for the home office while you have your business and there is no penalty in the form of lost capital gains exclusion later.

And finally, let's talk about the vacation home. Over the years, people have gotten creative in what counts as a vacation home. The IRS and Tax Court have settled on a definition that includes a dwelling with a kitchen and a bathroom. Recreational vehicles count. Boats may count. And, of course second residences count.

With the new Tax Act, we're now looking at limitations in the amounts that are deductible. Remember the mortgage interest deduction on up to $750,000 indebtedness includes both primary residence and vacation homes. And the $10,000 total limitation on the sum of state and local income tax and property tax applies to both your primary residence and vacation homes.

A lot of taxpayers are concerned about tax issues now with their vacation homes. What can be done to keep the deductions?

Strategy #24: *Turn your vacation home into a rental.* *There are three possible tax situations with a rental home. Each one has its own tax benefits and consequences.*

1. *Don't rent the home at all,*
2. *Rent the home for fewer than 15 days, or*
3. *Rent the home for more than 15 days.*

If you don't rent the home at all, then you have a second home. Your tax situation may have changed in 2018. Don't assume everything stayed the same.

If you use your vacation home for personal use for at least 15 days and rent it out for less than 15 days, the IRS will consider the primary function of the property to be personal. It is not a rental. Therefore, you don't report any rental income or losses.

In the case of the third example, you do need to report your rental income and expenses on Schedule E, just like any other rental.

If the property is still used for personal use, then you will need to allocate your property expenses between rental use and personal use. Any day that the property is not used for rental is considered personal use. Your costs such as mortgage interest, property tax, HOA dues and insurance will need to be allocated. Your utilities might also have to be allocated under the same formula if they can't be directly traced to rental use and personal use.

There is one more possibility. It is possible that the property becomes solely a rental property. If you have no personal use, the down time would count as rental days for expense allocation.

Chapter 4: Dependent Deductions

If you have dependents on your tax return, you're going to have changes in 2018.

Probably the biggest change is that you no longer have dependency exemptions. In fact, personal exemptions are all completely gone for 2018. No exemptions for your children. No exemptions for your elderly family members you are supporting.

In reality, other changes will cost you more, but this is one that is engrained in a lot of people's minds. Can I claim them on my tax return? Just count how many times you hear that question in contrast to other tax questions.

The personal exemption and dependency exemption may be gone, but there is now an expanded child tax credit to partially take its place. The tax credit phases out when your income exceeds $400,000 (married filing jointly) or $200,000 (single).

The name is a little misleading. For a limited time, adult children who are still full-time students or disabled and elderly relatives that qualify as dependents also will give you a small child tax credit.

And at the same time, the standard deduction has increased to $12,000, $16,000 or $24,000 (single, head of household, or married & filing jointly). There are strategy possibilities there!

Strategy #25: Children File Their Own Tax Returns. *If you have a child who currently works for you (or even outside the home), you might have wondered in the past whether you should still claim them as an exemption. Well, Congress has answered that question for you. You can no longer take that exemption because it doesn't exist anymore.*

And, at the same time, your child has a much bigger standard deduction when filing his or her own tax return. That means that he or she may be better off filing a separate return. You no longer can "claim" him or her for an exemption. Exemptions are gone.

If you have a business, this strategy gets even more powerful. You can pay your child a salary from your business for work they actually do and move income from your higher tax rate to his or her lower tax rate. If the income received is under $12,000, they won't even have any tax to pay.

With the money received by your child, they can pay education costs and other living expenses that you currently pay. In effect, the expenses you had been paying with after tax money are now being paid with untaxed money.

If you have a pass-through business structure, you may have considered changing some ownership over to your children. There could be a problem with that strategy. It's called the "kiddie tax."

The kiddie tax is applicable if:
1. The child's unearned income was more than $2,100,
2. The child meets one of the following age requirements:
    - The child was under age 18 at the end of the tax year,
    - The child was age 18 but less than 19 at the end of the tax year and the child's earned income didn't exceed one-half of the child's own support for the year (excluding scholarships if the child was a full-time student), or
    - The child was a full-time student who was at least 19 and under age 24 at the end of the tax year and the child's earned income didn't exceed one-half of the child's own support for the year (excluding scholarships)
3. At least one of the child's parents was alive at the end of the tax year
4. The child is required to file a tax return for the tax year, and
5. The child doesn't file a joint return for the tax year.

You may be asking "so what?" right now. The issue with the kiddie tax is that the unearned income (income from pass-through entities, interest, dividends, royalties or capital gains) will be taxed at trust tax return rates. In the past, the kiddie tax meant the child's unearned income was taxed at the parent's rates. Now, it's taxed at the higher trust tax rates. It's even more important to have a strategy for this.

The kiddie tax makes sure there is no tax benefit in moving unearned income to your children in this way. Don't set up portfolios for them. Don't give them part of your pass-through business. Or, if you do, prepare to have them pay more tax then you do.

Strategy #26: Pay Earned, Avoid Unearned. *Find a job for your child that is something he or she can reasonably do. A CPA in Florida won a case against the IRS when she put pictures of her baby daughter on her website and advertised herself as the "Family CPA." She paid her daughter a reasonable modeling fee for the work. The IRS challenged and she won!*

There are three rules I recommend that you follow if you pay your child from your business:
1. *Have a written job description,*
2. *Track hours of work or project completion if paid by the project, and*
3. *Pay a reasonable amount for the work actually done.*

The payment you pay your child, whether through payroll or as an independent contractor, is earned revenue. It's a deduction for your business and probably not even taxable for your child.

Don't make your child an owner in your business or investments. That creates unearned income which is taxed at the much higher trust tax rate. Find a job for him or her in your business instead.

As people are living longer and medical and housing costs increase, you may find yourself also having to support your parents or other older relatives. In that case, it might make more sense to give him or her a part of your business. The kiddie tax on unearned income is only an issue for minors. It's not an issue for older dependents or relatives.

Strategy #27: How to Move Income to an Adult Dependent. *In the case of an adult dependent, such as an elderly parent, the strategy to move some unearned income may make sense.*

For example, if you have a flow-through business with high income, you could make an elderly parent a partial shareholder. This would allow some of the income to move over to them so that they could pay for living expenses that you currently are paying with after tax money.

Before you put this strategy in place, make sure you discuss it with your CPA and possibly an estate tax planning attorney as well. When you give shares of a company to someone else, there could possibly be a taxable event, or at least a gift that may require a separate tax filing.

Additionally, you need to make arrangement to buy back or be given the shares upon the death of your elderly relative. It may also create an issue if later the relative
wanted to qualify for a state Medicaid program.

Like with most strategies, you need to carefully consider the ramifications of the action taken.

Additional Uses for 529 Plans

The Trump Tax Plan also added some provisions to the independent school sector. One, in particular is a major change to how Section 529 plans are treated.

A 529 plan is a tax-advantaged method of saving for future educational expenses that is authorized by Section 529 of the Internal Revenue Code. Originally, the 529 Plan was set up to provide for college expenses only. The plan allows an account holder to establish an educational savings account for a beneficiary and use the money to pay for tuition, room and board, mandatory fees and required books and computers. The money contributed to the account can be invested in stocks, bonds, mutual funds or in money market funds. The earnings are not subject to federal tax (or state tax, in most cases) as long as the money is used only for qualified educational expenses. The plans are
open to both adults and children.

Under the new law, Section 529 plans are allowed to distribute up to $10,000 in expenses for tuition incurred in connection with enrollment or attendance to a public, private or religious elementary or secondary school. This limitation is applied on a per-student basis, not on a per-account basis. Thus, if an individual is a designated beneficiary of multiple accounts, the most the individual may receive is $10,000, free of tax.

50

The new provision is silent related to whether or not funding for 2018 distributions must occur after Dec. 31, 2017. It appears that existing balances in section 529 plans may be used as qualifying distributions in 2018, it is just that the distributions need to be addressed for these kinds of expenses.

The Act also tells us that expenses for curriculum, curricular materials, books or instructional materials, online education materials, tuition, tutoring or educational classes outside of the home (but only if the tutor or instructor is not related), dual enrollment in an institution of higher education and educational therapies for students with disabilities, in connection with a home school will qualify.

Strategy #28: States Sweeten the Pot for 529 Plans. When you make a contribution to a 529 plan, you don't receive a federal tax deduction or tax credit. But you may get a state tax deduction or credit. In fact, it's easier to list the states where you don't get a credit or deduction. Those states are: Alaska, California, Delaware, Florida, Hawaii, Kentucky, Maine, Nevada, New Hampshire, New Jersey, North Carolina, South Dakota, Tennessee, Texas, Washington and Wyoming. Every other state and the District of Columbia offer some kind of benefit.

In the past, Section 529 plans could only be used for higher education. With the Tax Cuts and Jobs Act, the funds can be withdrawn for all kinds of education including private schools and home schooling programs.

The strategy here is specifically for people whose children go to private schools or who are enrolled in a qualified home school. Make a contribution to their 529 plan, take the state deduction or tax credit and then take the money out of the plan to pay for the school.

Summing Up Individual Tax Changes

We've just covered some significant changes to how individual taxes will work, starting in 2018. We're not quite at the postcard-sized return, as discussed by some politicians, but the individual tax return bulk has been greatly reduced for many people. There were a lot of deductions for individuals that were lost. That's why we have to look beyond normal strategies from here on out.

In fact, Section 2 is going to give you the biggest overall strategy. Are you ready to step up to more income, financial control and less taxes, so you end up with more cash? One more chapter and we'll be there.

Chapter 5: Individual & Investment Tax Strategies for 2018 & Beyond

There have been a lot of changes in tax strategies, particularly for individual tax returns. In fact, right now, you might feel a little overwhelmed with the 28 strategies we've talk about so far. Some of them are very specific strategies based on special circumstances that might not be applicable for you.

If you're wondering, "Okay, great, but how do I pay less tax?" then this is the chapter for you! We'll keep the strategies clear and straightforward!

For Individuals: Strategies That Work Now
If you set up a one-on-one consultation with me, I am going to tell you the truth. Some things will work. Some things will not, no matter what other so-called experts tell you. That's especially true if they are trying to sell you something.

I recently had a consultation with a couple who had some big dreams and were doing all the wrong things to get there. The laws have changed. At the end, they weren't happy with the news I had to share. They had counted on a storybook ending, but wanted to use only paper assets and cryptocurrency to get there. Let's look at what happened a little more in depth.

Coming soon! *Tax Loopholes for Crypto* releases September 2018. It explains what we know about crypto and taxes and what we don't know. The IRS has given some guidance, but not a lot. This is where you need a CPA with experience to help guide you through the best strategies, based on experience with other similar investments and businesses.

Tax Loopholes for Crypto will be available at Amazon in printed book form and through Kindle September 2018.

Paper Investments Tax Strategies
There are three types of investments that an individual may make:

1. Real estate investments,
2. Owned businesses, and
3. Paper assets.

Paper assets are stocks, bonds, mutual funds and the like. These are the kind of assets where you buy a small part of them and generally receive cash flow through dividends or interest or by selling the asset.

In the past, you had investment expense deductions that were allowed. These were things like advisor fees, subscriptions to financial publications, online research subscriptions, online services to manage investments, transportation to your broker's or investment advisor's office, safe deposit box fee to store certificates, cost to replace lost certificates, and attorney, legal and bookkeeping fees to produce and collect investment income.

Those expenses are still deductible up to limitations based on your AGI with your 2017 tax return.

After that, effective January 1, 2018, they are not deductible for income tax purposes.

Strategy #29: Realize the Advantages & Disadvantages of Paper Assets. *The best deductions and tax advantages come with a business. The second best tax advantages will come with real estate investments. That's made better if you or your spouse (if married, filing jointly) is a real estate professional. The worst, practically, non existent, tax advantages come with paper assets.*

If you want to build your wealth solely with paper assets and a job, you'll need to save more money because you don't have tax advantages working with you. The best strategy is to have a side business (or full-time business) and invest in real estate. That way, you can take advantage of tax breaks to help you grow wealth faster.

Investment Expense and Medicare Surcharge
Strangely, investment expenses ARE deductible for determining the Medicare Surcharge of 3.8%. This Medicare Surcharge is assessed on net investment income (investment income less allowable investment expenses) if your modified adjusted gross income is over $200,000 if

you're single, or over $250,000 if you're married filing jointly.

Your modified adjusted gross income is your adjusted gross income (AGI) with the following deductions, where applicable:
- Student loan interest
- One-half of self-employment tax
- Qualified tuition expenses
- Tuition and fees deduction
- Passive loss or passive income
- IRA contributions
- Taxable social security payments
- The exclusion of income from U.S. savings bonds
- The exclusion for adoption expenses
- Rental losses
- Any overall loss from a publicly traded partnership

Investment Interest
You can still deduct investment interest expenses against your investment income when calculating your taxable income from investments.

But other than that, your deductions just were reduced.

The best wealth building and tax saving strategy is to create an asset that will grow in value, give you cash flow and give you a tax break. Hit all three of those and you have a winner!

Since deductions have been largely eliminated for individuals, there really are only 2 ways to win at this and that's with either a business or with real estate investments.

The strategy here? Paper investments may work as part of an overall investment strategy, but for tax strategies, you're better off with a business. Real estate investments are better than paper assets too. Remember that if your income is above the $150,000 adjusted gross income threshold, you can't take real estate tax losses against your other income. If you (or your spouse if married, filing jointly) are a qualified real estate professional, real estate tax losses are considered nonpassive and will be deductible against your other income.

Cryptocurrency Investments
The only thing more confusing (and disappointing) than the new rules on investment deductions are the IRS's rules on cryptocurrency investments.

The Trump Tax Plan did have one change that insiders feel was targeted at cryptocurrencies. The Tax Code regarding like-kind exchanges of property was clarified to mean real property. In other words, real estate is covered under the Section 1031, like-kind exchange rules. Cryptocurrencies are not.

If you "exchange" one type of crypto for another type, it is not a tax-deferred exchange. It is actually sale and a purchase. The gain or loss on the sale would be reported as a short or long term capital gain or loss, depending on how long you held the currency. The basis for the newly purchased currency is the value at the time you exchanged or purchased it. The start day for the purchase is the day of the exchange.

Strategy #30: Exchanges Aren't Exchanges When It Comes to Crypto. *This is very misunderstood in the cryptocurrency world right now. Effective January 1, 2018, if you "exchange" one cryptocurrency for another type, you have a taxable event. Make sure you plan for the tax if you make this type of transaction.*

Unexpected Tax When You Buy Products or Services
If you use your crypto currency to buy products or services, the IRS treats the use of your crypto as a sale. That means you'll have to report the sale for either short or long- term capital gains or losses.

The amount of gain or loss is determined by the "sales" price or the value of that crypto on the day used to purchase the product or service less your basis. The short or long term nature of the gain or loss is determined based on how long you held the crypto. If you held it for 1 year or less, it is short term. If it is more than 1 year, it is long term.

Strategy #31: Crypto is NOT Currency. *The biggest shock to many cryptocurrency investors is that the IRS does not treat cryptocurrency as currency. If you use crypto to buy a product or service, it is treated as if you sold it and had gain or loss.*

The biggest strategy here is realizing that you have a taxable event. Before you use a crypto to purchase a product or service, make sure you factor in the amount of tax you'll have to pay.

Crypto "Dividends"

Sometimes cryptocurrencies pay out dividends. Only, you may not realize that's what is happening.

For example, in 2017, Bitcoin gave all holders on record as of a certain date a new currency, Bitcoin Cash. Most people thought, "Awesome" and went on their way. They didn't realize that a taxable event had just occurred.

The value of Bitcoin Cash as of the date that it was given is considered ordinary income. It is not taxed at the special capital gains and dividend tax rate. It's taxed at the higher ordinary income tax rate.

Coinbase tracks Bitcoin owners of record. And the IRS recently won a case that forced Coinbase to turn over their records. The IRS is going down the list to make sure everyone on it is reporting their transactions. Otherwise, they ask why. And they might not be very nice when they ask.

You're not invisible.

Cryptocurrency Summary

Let's summarize the above regarding cryptocurrency:

Cryptos are considered intangible property. When you buy crypto, it is not an expense. It's an asset with a basis. Remember, you do not get a tax deduction when you purchase assets.

When you use crypto to buy a product or service, it is considered a sale of the crypto. You need to report a sale based on the fair market value of the crypto as of that day.

If you "exchange" one crypto for another, you actually have a sale of the crypto and then a purchase of the other one (not deductible). It is reportable for tax purposes. You cannot do a tax free exchange of cryptos.

If there is a "dividend" paid in the form of a spin-off or other crypto (hard or soft fork), it is taxable as ordinary income.

Cryptocurrency speculation is not a tax-advantaged investment. It may make you money, provided you buy and sell right, but it's also going to be taxed every step of the way. There are a few strategies for this, though, and that's what *Tax Loopholes for Crypto*, releasing September 2018 discusses.

Back to My Unhappy Consultation Client
This is the part where my consultation with my prospective client fell apart. The couple were high income W-2 wage earners. Their itemized deductions were phasing out. They didn't want to hear that 2017 was the best it was ever going to be for them, at least as it applied to tax strategies. They lived in a high tax state and their state income tax deduction was going to be limited to $10,000. They wouldn't get any real estate property tax deduction. Or, if they did, they would lose most of their state income tax deduction.

They would have no unreimbursed job expense deductions.

They needed a new tax strategy.

They didn't want a new tax strategy.

Somewhere they had gotten the idea that purchases of cryptocurrency were tax deductions. They're not. They are investments. In this case, it's like buying a stock or bond. You don't get a deduction when you buy them. (That didn't change with the

Trump Tax Plan. Buying an asset has never been a deduction.)

Unlike the special tax rate you get when a stock pays you a dividend, you have to pay regular, ordinary tax rate for the dividend that a crypto pays. And when a crypto gives you more cryptos, like Bitcoin did with Bitcoin Cash, it's taxable. And you pay tax at the ordinary tax rate.

At the end of our call, when I told them their plan wouldn't work, and what they needed to do instead, they told me how unhappy they were with the consultation. They wanted to be told that their plan WOULD work. They could keep their high income jobs. They could keep all of their deductions. They could deduct the cost of the cryptocurrency they bought and never pay tax when they sold it. And my answer was, "Nope."

If you want the truth, call me. If you want a tax-saving, asset-protecting, cash flow-creating, wealth-expanding strategy that will work, call me. If you want me to buy into your fairy tale, please do us both a favor. Don't call.

Cryptocurrency Mining is a Business
Crypto mining, on the other hand, is a business. The value that is reported as income is the fair market value of the crypto created as of the date of its creation. This also becomes the basis for determining gain when you sell. The expenses are the operating expenses for the business.

Non-reimbursed Job Expenses
Some jobs require a lot of extra work and expense on the employee's part. For example, sales people may be required to pick up their meals expense when traveling for the business and their vehicle expenses. Medical professionals may be required to pay for their own education. Union workers may have to pay for their own union dues.

In the past, those were a deduction for the employee. These are no longer deductible for the employee as that deduction no longer exists.

Strategy #32: Save Your Job Related Expense Deductions. If your boss won't allow you to become an independent contractor, start a small side business that allows you take the same type of write-offs. Remember in order for you have a legitimate business deduction, you need to show that the expense is ordinary and necessary for the type of business. You also have to be able to prove that you have a legitimate business. It's not an ideal strategy, starting a business just for the write-offs, but you may find a business that you enjoy and makes money for you and provides for your future.

Overall, the Tax Cuts and Jobs Act has not been a friend to individual taxpayers and investors who strictly invest in paper assets. If that describes you, the best strategy is to take a hard look at what the tax bill will mean to you. Don't assume that your employer is withholding enough tax to cover your expenses. In fact, if you're in one of the high state income tax states or high real estate tax states, you are almost certainly under withholding your taxes. That means you'll owe a whole lot more in taxes when it comes tax time.

This is a case where forewarned is forearmed, provided, of course, that you take action to change your circumstances.

Section II: Start a Business

Chapter 6: Why Start a Business?

You may have heard the laments. "The middle class lost the ability to deduct state taxes. The rich still have that deduction!" "The middle class can't deduct casualty losses, but the rich can!" Name a deduction that was lost on your individual tax return and chances are there is an article that will say it's not fair and that only the poor and middle class lost it.

The reality is that it's not a case of rich versus poor or even rich versus middle-class. It's a case of businesses owners vs. employees. The choice is really quite simple. Which side of this equation do you want to be on?

You can start a business tonight (yes, it really is that simple) and have the deductions that the new Tax Act preserved for businesses and has taken away from individuals.

In the next few chapters, we're going to look at what it takes to be a legitimate business in the eyes of the IRS and why that is so important. We're also going to look at some possible suggestions for a business, if you're brand new to entrepreneurship.

If you already have a business, don't skip over this section. You will find fundamental strategies that work for any business, new or seasoned. Plus, you may find that you want to start a new business. More on that later.

Why Does Having a Business Provide Tax Savings?
Ever think that tax laws aren't fair and equal?

Guess what.... They're not!

Big business can afford lobbyists to make sure they continue to get the tax breaks. That's why there were so many versions of the Tax Cuts and Job Act before it was finalized. There were a lot of compromises along the way. By and large, though, the compromises were in favor of big businesses.

But there is a secret advantage. And it's an advantage any average W-2 employee can use! You can take advantage of those very same tax breaks, as long as you follow the rules.

When it comes to tax breaks:

Big Business = Small Business

The Trump Tax Plan is no different from other legislation. Business owners get the benefits. But if you ever find yourself thinking it's not fair, that's right. The tax system is rigged. The most important fact, though, is that you can move from employee status to business owner status quickly. All you need to do is -

Start a business.

Strategy #33: Follow the Tax Laws and See Where They Go.
Tax laws are written for business owners and real estate investors. If you don't have a business, start one. Make sure it's a business in the eyes of the IRS. If you have year after year of loss in your business, the IRS may try to call it just your hobby. A hobby gain (income is higher than expenses) means that you will have to pay tax. A hobby loss is not deductible. Getting the "hobby" designation is something
you want to avoid.

Once you've ascertained you have a legitimate business in the eyes of the IRS, look for all the deductions you can take. You'll see that there are often expenses you have right now that are really hidden business deductions. These aren't additional expenses, but items that you paid for previously with after tax money. Now, they can be paid with before tax money because they are deductible.

More than anything, it's a mindset change. Look at everything you spend money on and ask, "How could this be a hidden business tax deduction?"

Why start a business? It's more than just for the tax savings, or should be. You can create a future for yourself and your family. Maybe right now you can't see ever replacing your job. That's okay. Maybe a business means $500 extra money a month. When you consider the tax savings that would be a lot more. What difference could that make? You can teach your children essential business skills as they work alongside you to build the business. Although this book is focusing on tax strategies, there is a lot more than just tax to consider when it comes to taking charge of your financial future.

Strategy #34: Find your hidden business deductions. *The IRS code at Section 162 tells us that a business deduction must be ordinary and necessary to the production of income in order to be deductible. That's actually pretty subjective, when you think about it. Each business type will have different types of deductions. I like to start with first discovering where your money goes.*

When you call us to schedule a consultation, we'll send out a questionnaire. You can complete all of it, part of it or none of it. The one thing I do need is to know what topics you want to discuss. What are your tax, asset protection, financial, business building, cash flow creation, etc. questions? The more information I receive, though, the better job I can do for you. One of the things that's included in the package is 'Where does your money go?"

Why is this important to you? This strategy is to find your hidden business deductions.

Once you've identified where your money is spent, not where you think it is going, but actually where it is spent, you can then go through expenses with me to find the possible deductions.

Here are the top 5 items that I've discovered over the years with my clients. Remember these are the personal expenses that can possibly be business deductions.

#1: Your home. Almost every business owner I've met does some work at home, even if he or she has another business location. If that space is used regularly and exclusively for business purpose, you have a deduction. Now, post the new Tax Act, it's become even more important because you may be picking up deductions that Congress and the IRS won't let you take otherwise.

#2: Auto. If you have business use of your vehicle, you have some kind of auto deduction. It could be based on the mileage method (cents per mile) or it could be based on the percentage of business use. If you get the percentage use, you apply that percentage multiplied by the interest carrying cost (if any), depreciation, gas,

oil, tires, repairs, insurance and the like to determine your deductible expense. You can
only take one (mileage) or the other (percentage), not both.

If you buy a "heavy vehicle", defined as a vehicle that has a GVWR of 6,000 lbs. or more, you can also take a Section 179 deduction of $25,000. If you have less than 100% business use, just multiply the business use percentage by $25,000. You also get bonus depreciation.

In most cases with the new tax law, it has become more advantageous to buy a vehicle, rather than lease. Check with your tax advisor to crunch the numbers. Or you can register your book at our website, following the instructions in Chapter 16, to join our private forum and we can run some numbers there.

#3: Kids. To be clear, usually it's the school and sports expenses that taxpayers wonder about.

There are generally two strategies that are helpful. Can you pay your child for work they legitimately do in your business? If so, your child can receive income and pay tax at a low or zero tax rate and you get a tax deduction for your business. Then your child starts paying some of those expenses you currently pay with after tax money.

Once your child becomes an employee, there may be classes that are applicable for the work he or she does for the business. For example, if your child helps you with your website, then a computer camp expense would be a deduction for the business.

You probably can't write off everything but you can likely reduce your taxes with these strategies.

One more item, there are three things I recommend you do if you employ your child:

1. You must have a written job description,
2. You must pay a reasonable wage for the work done, and
3. You (or your child) must keep track of the hours.

#4 Meals. Post Tax Act, the meals and entertainment deductions have changed for businesses.

If you have a meal at a place of employment (including your home office) and for the benefit of the employer, your meal will be 50% deductible. It used to be 100%, but it has been reduced in 2018 and will eventually phase out completely.

If you have a meal outside the office for benefit of the business (with customers, employees, vendors, prospects, etc.), the cost is 50% deductible.

Entertainment is not deductible at all. An example of that might be renting a Skybox to entertain prospects. The idea is that you want them to become customers at some point, but it is entertainment, not a meal, and so it's not deductible.

#5 Travel. If you travel for business, it's partially or fully deductible. Here are some scenarios that might apply for you.

1. *You travel for 3 days of business and 2 days of fun. If the "fun days" are in the beginning of the work time, then your hotel stay during the whole time will be deductible. The meals on the fun days aren't deductible. The meals on the work days will be. If you do some other things for fun, like you see a Broadway show in New York City while you're there for business, the cost of the tickets won't be deductible.*
2. *You travel for 3 days of business and 2 days of fun. In this case, the fun days are at the end of your stay. You actually could leave, so it's not necessary to stay. The cost of your staying in the travel city for that extra time is not deductible. But, the cost of the travel is fully deductible.*
3. *If your travel is international, you will need to allocate your travel costs (air fare, etc.) between work days and fun days. You do not have the same requirement for domestic travel.*

What is work-related travel? It's travel you take when you work. It could mean that you're talking to potential or existing vendors, prospects, customers, or checking out the competition. You also could have an annual Board of Directors meeting for your company. Keep your minutes to prove that you were there for business purposes.

Those are just examples of things that could be deductible.

Does it Deduct?

At live seminars, I sometimes go through an exercise with people in the audience called "Does it deduct?" Attendees call out personal expenses they currently have and then once I have a list, we go through and think of how this expense could be a legitimate business deduction.

In order to be a deduction, the expense must be ordinary and necessary to the production of income.

At one such seminar, we went through the usual expenses like kids, home, school, car, travel, software, computers and the like. And then one guy asked if he could deduct his bed.

Silence.

As I reminded everyone, the bed would have to be an ordinary and necessary expense for the production of business income. I finally just said that there are some things that won't be deductible, or if they are, we can't talk about it in a family program.

But, the dog as someone else questioned could be a deduction. The dog may be part of your advertising. He could be part of your brand, mainly if you have a pet food company, dog training company, dog accessory company or something similar. Or, he could provide security. In all of those cases, you could deduct the cost of the dog, pet food, vet bills or other dog-related expenses.

One of the huge benefits of having a business is the deductions you can take. For the most part, these have stayed the same after the Tax Act. Entertainment expenses are gone and if you have a large company (defined as a company with average annual gross revenues of $25,000,000 or more) your interest expense will be limited. There are some other changes which we discuss later in Section 3. However, for the most part, it's a matter of determining what is deductible. How can this expense be ordinary and necessary to the production of income? What can you deduct?

What If Your Business Has a Loss?
Your business will have direct expenses that are directly related to the

production of income (hence, the name). For example, if you sell products online, you have the cost of those goods and that is a direct expense against the sales price. If you sell professional services and have employees who help you provide those services, your costs of goods are the salaries, taxes and benefits for the people who do the work.

You will also have some expenses that are general & administrative costs and, in some cases, were actually personal expenses in the beginning. For example, you may have a personal residence that you had before your business. You convert some of the home into a home office so that you have a headquarters for your new business. Costs associated with the home office are a deduction, even though for the most part they were costs that you had before you had the business.

When you add up all those deductions, chances are your business will show a loss in the beginning few years. The next question is whether that loss will be deductible. There are two things to remember if you have a business loss. You need to have active participation and you need to have sufficient basis.

There are two types of basis you may have for your business: equity basis and debt basis. Equity basis is compromised of the money you put into the business for equity. For example, it's the amount you paid for the stock in your S Corporation or C Corporation. It could be the amount you paid for member units in an LLC or partner units in a Partnership. If you just started up the business with very little money and bootstrapped the growth, by reinvesting profits, you will show very little initial equity in the business.

Debt basis is the total of the money you have lent to the business and, in the case of a partnership, the amount of debt that the business may have incurred and which you have personally guaranteed. If you personally guarantee debt for a corporation, you do not receive debt basis.

If you don't have sufficient equity basis and/or debt basis, losses you may receive from the flow-through business structures will not be personally deductible.

Before the end of the year, review your strategy for writing off business losses if those are anticipated.

Strategy #35: Create Basis Prior to Loss. *If you don't have enough basis to deduct a business loss from a pass-through entity, take a look at why you don't have the basis. This is often due to loans that your business has taken that created cash in the business but were not personally guaranteed so did not increase your basis. One possible strategy, in the case of a partnership, would be for you to personally guarantee the loans. If you have recourse financing in a partnership, this will increase your basis. It also means that you are personally liable for the debt so it may be something you want to consider carefully before you just sign on the dotted line.*

In the case of an S Corporation, if you personally guarantee the debt, it doesn't increase your debt basis. A strategy here would be to get the loan personally and then personally loan the money to the S Corporation. The Corporation owes you, not a third party. That means you have created additional debt basis.

S Corporation Owners Double Up Taxes

The main concern of one of my consultation clients was why his taxes were so high.

He and his wife owned a handful of successful burger franchises, which they operated through an S Corporation. I would have preferred to see the different burger stores held in separate S Corporations, but that is for asset protection,
not for any tax benefit.

The biggest question still remained, why were their taxes so high?

S Corporations are pass-through entities. The S Corporation return reports the income and expenses, but the total net income or loss is reported on the individual tax returns of the owners. In this case, the only owners were the husband and wife and they filed together on their married, filing joint return.

The S Corporation showed a loss. Initially that was a surprise because

I knew that it had been successful for the owners. It could be that this particular year was an anomaly, or it could be that I needed to keep looking.

I kept looking.

I saw that they had taken large salaries out of the S Corporation. That income was a deduction for the S Corporation and was reported as W-2 income on their personal return. In this case, they took a salary of $250,000 each, for a total of $500,000. The salaries were higher than the income in the S Corporation before their salaries so there was a loss in the S Corporation of approximately $200,000.

In essence, that meant that their S Corporation made about $300,000 ($500,000 - $200,000). But they paid tax on the full $500,000. The $200,000 loss from the S Corporation was not reported.

What happened?

The problem was that the owners did not have sufficient basis in their S Corporation. That meant they could not deduct the loss on their return. It was suspended. However, they did have to report the $500,000 in salaries. They should have paid tax on $300,000, in some combination of salary and income from the S Corporation. Instead, they paid tax on the full $500,000.

The solution in this case was to reduce their salary so that there was a profit, not loss, in the S Corporation. The income from the S Corporation could then be offset by the suspended carryover losses from previous years.

And, moving forward, the salary amount that should be paid has to be more carefully strategized and monitored. It's best if an S Corporation owner takes a salary and distribution, which represents some of the income from the S Corp. You'll pay less payroll taxes because of the lower salary and now with the Tax Cuts and Jobs Act flow-through income reduction, you'll pay less income taxes as well.

More on all that coming up!

Chapter 7: Sure You Think You Have a Business, But Does the IRS Agree?

After the last chapter, I hope you realize how a business can help you save taxes and keep money in your pocket. Now here is the real warning.

If you don't meet the IRS's guidelines for a REAL business, you can kiss all those business deductions good-bye.

It doesn't matter if you have good records, you don't get any deductions if you don't have an IRS-friendly business. It doesn't matter if you keep awesome travel logs, there still are no deductions without an IRS-friendly business. It doesn't matter if you have every receipt ever written and can prove it helped you in your business, if you don't meet these IRS guidelines, there are no deductions for you.

The secret is simple. Make sure you have an IRS-Friendly business so you can get all the tax breaks.

The IRS has created a 9 Factor test to find out how IRS-Friendly your business really is.

This boils down to four categories. Pass this test and you have an IRS-friendly business that allows you to take deductions. If you fail the test, the IRS is going to disallow your deductions and charge you tax, penalties and interest. The simplest, first pass, is to look at these four categories.

The IRS targets certain types of businesses, such as home-based businesses, horse ranches, and auto racing more than others. The reason that home-based businesses are targeted is because so many people start them and then never do anything with the business. If the business is profitable, it doesn't matter. But, in the beginning years, it often isn't clear whether you are just starting on the road to a successful business or are not really taking the business seriously.

In the other cases, horses, dogs and racing cars for example, the IRS is looking for hobbies that people are trying to write-off. Of course, you could have a ramped up hobby that actually is a business but you need to pass the IRS test to prove it.

How IRS-Friendly Is Your Business?

Category #1:   Business-like Manner
A good way to prove this is by having a separate checking account, keeping good records and having a business plan. A business these days has a website and/or a Facebook page. Depending on the business, you may also have an Instagram page. And, of course, Twitter and Linked-In are important social media outlets as well. The key is to make sure you can prove you are marketing your business like a business.

You also should have regular financial statements that you review. If you're losing money, you need to show that you're trying different things to make the business profitable.

It doesn't have to be profitable yet, you just need to demonstrate that you're seriously working to turn it into a successful profitable business.

Category #2: Experience
The IRS is going to ask if you've been successful in a similar business in the past. If you haven't, they're going to ask who your advisor, leader, mentor and/or coach is. And then they'll ask you if that person (or persons) has had or is currently having a success in business. But it doesn't stop there. They'll also ask if you attend classes or webinars, have read books or otherwise studied about your business. If you continue to learn more about your business and if, as a result, your sales are increasing, you have a good case to prove that you are actively trying to make it profitable.

Category #3: Time and Effort
A lot of businesses start out as part-time endeavors. That's part of the reason why so many people can get involved. A part-time or side business doesn't require the full-time commitment of money and

time that a regular business does, especially when there is often no source of other income. Bootstrapping, building the business yourself with your resources, can be the safest way to start.

But that doesn't mean you can build your business by doing nothing. Every business needs you to do something.

The IRS will want to see that you're putting in the necessary time to build your business. In the past, they've said that 2 days per week and one or two weekends a month was sufficient to prove you were putting in the time and effort.

And now we come to the real challenge.

Category # 4: Profit
If you have a profit in your business, after all legitimate, properly recorded deductions, then the IRS is going to give you a "pass" on this test. But if you have a loss, then the IRS wants to be sure that you're serious. That's why they have the first three tests. But that isn't enough. They want to know that:
1. You've had profit in the past from similar businesses,
2. You have had occasional profit in this business, and/or
3. You've got a clear-cut plan how you will make it profitable.

Strategy #36: Strongly Make Your Case for an IRS-Friendly Business *If you have a loss in your business, take the time to run through the 4 categories, at a minimum. If your business loss goes on for several years, the IRS may challenge you that you actually have a hobby, not a business. Hobby losses are not deductible.*

If you have a problem with any of these categories, it's most likely going to be Category 4. If that's true for you, make sure you're especially strong in the other 3 categories. Prove you are operating like a real business and that you're putting in the necessary time and effort to make a go of it. And, get some help when you need it. That way you can show you are trying to improve your business future.

There is one big exception to having a profit motive in your business. Or at least, the profit motive as you're probably thinking of it.

If your business builds assets, that counts as the profit motive.

This is how some businesses have been able to continue for years, running at a loss. They are building out an application, establishing value for IP or building a brand. For example, Amazon ran losses for years until they went public. And now, they are a huge success story. The IRS never challenged the fact that they were a real business.

Why Is Any of This Important?

In the beginning with your business, you will have direct expenses. These are expenses directly related to sales of products or your services. The indirect expenses are general & administrative expenses and often, especially in the beginning, are hidden business deductions that had previously been personal expenses.

In the beginning, the direct expenses are usually covered by the sales in the business. If not, that is something you'll need to check on quickly. Indirect expenses, though, may not be covered, so you have a loss. But remember a lot of these expenses were personal expenses before, so it's a tax advantage to have that loss.

Well, it's almost a tax advantage. If you don't take the deduction against other income, there really is no advantage.

And that's where the IRS comes into play. If they decide you have a hobby and not a business, then your loss is not deductible against other income. If you have income in a hobby, you have to pay tax. But a hobby loss gives you no advantage.

That's why it is so important to have your business qualified as a business under the IRS's guidelines. If you do, you get the business loss tax advantage.

Because the IRS Says It's So!

There are a number of ways to determine what the IRS's position is going to be on a certain item. You can look directly at the Code. That will give you a broad-brush approach. The Treasury Regulations show more detail and the 'how-to' of how to approach the subject.

There are also Revenue Regulations, Revenue Rulings and Tax Court cases to consider.

Now we're going to look at the Treasury Regulation that specifically addresses the entire subject of being in business. The asset exception is at Treasury Regulation Sec 1.183-2 (b) (4). This states:

(4) Expectation that assets used in activity may appreciate in value. The term profit encompasses appreciation in the value of assets, such as land, used in the activity. Thus, the taxpayer may intend to derive a profit from the operation of the activity, and may also intend that, even if no profit from current operations is derived, an overall profit will result when appreciation in the value of land used in the activity is realized since income from the activity together with the appreciation of land will exceed expenses of operation. See, however, paragraph (d) of §1.183–1 for definition of an activity in this connection.

Treasury Regulation Sec 1.183-1 (d) states:

d) Activity defined—(1) Ascertainment of activity. In order to determine whether, and to what extent, section 183 and the regulations thereunder apply, the activity or activities of the taxpayer must be ascertained. For instance, where the taxpayer is engaged in several undertakings, each of these may be a separate activity, or several undertakings may constitute one activity. In ascertaining the activity or activities of the taxpayer, all the facts and circumstances of the case must be taken into account. Generally, the most significant facts and circumstances in making this determination are the degree of organizational and economic interrelationship of various undertakings, the business purpose which is (or might be) served by carrying on the various undertakings separately or together in a trade or business or in an investment setting, and the similarity of various undertakings. Generally, the Commissioner will accept the characterization by the taxpayer of several undertakings either as a single activity or as separate activities. The taxpayer's characterization will not be accepted, however, when it appears that his characterization is artificial and cannot be reasonably supported under the facts and circumstances of the case. If the taxpayer engages in two or more separate activities, deductions and income from each separate activity are not aggregated either in determining whether a particular activity is engaged in for profit or in applying section 183. Where land is purchased or held primarily with the intent to profit from increase in its value, and the taxpayer also engages in farming on such land, the farming and the holding of the land will ordinarily be considered a single activity only if the farming activity reduces the net cost of carrying the land for its appreciation in value. Thus, the farming and holding of the land will be considered a single activity only if the income derived from farming exceeds the deductions attributable to the farming activity which are not directly attributable to the holding of the land (that is, deductions other than those directly attributable to the holding of the land such as interest on a mortgage secured by the land, annual property taxes attributable to the land and improvements, and depreciation of improvements to the land).

The IRS ATG (audit handbook) states the following regarding the asset appreciation exception:

The term "profit" encompasses appreciation in the value of assets used in the activity. Thus, the taxpayer may intend to derive a profit from the operation of the activity, and may also intend that even if no profit when appreciation in the value of the land used in the activity realized since income from the activity together with appreciation of land will exceed expenses of operation.

List assets used in the activity.
- *Were the assets held prior to starting the business?*
- *Was depreciation previously taken as a deduction?*
- *What was the prior use?*
- *How and when were the assets acquired (verify taxpayer's basis)?*
- *Are any assets used personally?*
- *How much is each asset worth today?*
- *Has anyone ever offered to buy any of the assets?*
- *Is it likely the assets will appreciate in value?*
- *Why does the taxpayer expect the appreciation to occur?*
- *At what rate are assets expected to appreciate?*
- *Over what period of time (how many years)?*
- *What are the taxpayer's plans for the appreciated asset(s)?*
- *At what point does the taxpayer intend to realize the inherent gain for tax purposes?*
- *Will the gain on appreciated assets offset operating losses – to the extent that the overall net result on the business is a profit?*

- The IRS may question taxpayers regarding whether an activity is a business or a hobby. If the activity is not engaged in for profit, it is subject to the hobby loss rules in Sec. 183, and its deductible expenses are limited to the amount of income it generates, further subject to a threshold of 2% of adjusted gross income (AGI) as a miscellaneous itemized deduction. (This is no longer allowed starting January 1, 2018.)

In the right circumstances, the fact that you are growing assets can be very powerful.

These 4 categories are a general breakdown. For more detail, let's look at the 9 factors or questions specifically.

Regs. Sec. 1.183-2(b) lists nine factors for determining whether a taxpayer engages in an activity for profit:

1. **How the taxpayer carries on the activity.** A tax preparer would first want to look for how the taxpayer handles the entity, ensuring that he or she is conducting all activities in a businesslike manner. The taxpayer can establish this by maintaining separate personal and business bank accounts, keeping records and books, and acting like similar profitable, operational entities.
2. **The taxpayer's expertise.** A business operator should have extensive knowledge of his or her profession or activity, showing that he or she has studied accepted business methods and sought advice from experts.
3. **The taxpayer's time and effort in carrying out the activity.**
    - *Example.* J manages a janitorial service, and his prime contract is with a fast-food chain. J also teaches three days a week at a local university and can clean the restaurants only late in the evening after closing or early in the morning before opening. This causes him to devote much of his personal time and effort to cleaning, which could indicate that he entered into and continued it with the actual and honest objective of making a profit.

4. **An expectation that assets used in an activity, such as land, may appreciate in value.** Regs. Sec. 1.183-2(b)(4) says such appreciation may be considered in lieu of current profits.
5. **The taxpayer's success in other activities.** Even if the taxpayer's activity is currently unprofitable, it may be for-profit if the taxpayer has been able to convert other activities from unprofitable to profitable in the past, especially ones similar to the current activity.
6. **The taxpayer's history of income or losses from the activity.** The economy plays a big role in how much business the hypothetical janitor can generate and keep. Since *J*'s main contract is with a fast-food chain whose budget fluctuates with the economy, he sometimes incurs losses, which alone are not conclusive. However, a long series of losses warrants consideration, and sustained earnings indicate a for-profit activity.
7. **The relative amounts of the profits and losses.** Regulation. Sec. 1.183-2(b)(7) states, "The amount of profits in relation to the amount of losses incurred, and in relation to the amount of the taxpayer's investment and the value of the assets used in the activity, may provide useful criteria in determining the taxpayer's intent." However, the presumption of profit motive in Sec. 183(d) says that if an activity has gross income for three or more of the last five years that exceeds the deductions attributable to the activity, the activity generally is presumed to be for-profit.
8. **The taxpayer's financial status.** Although other substantial sources of income to the taxpayer do not preclude an activity from being considered for-profit, they may indicate the activity is a hobby. In the example, *J* also teaches three days per week at a local university during the academic year. He is not paid when school is not in session. During those months, he relies solely on his janitorial business for income. *J*'s janitorial services can be considered a for-profit activity whether or not school is in session.
9. **Whether the activity provides recreation or involves "personal motives."** This may, with other factors, indicate lack of a profit motive. *J*'s janitorial service entails cleaning

grills, mopping floors, and scrubbing public bathrooms. The activity lacks recreational appeal, helping J's business to be seen as a for-profit activity rather than a hobby.

After reviewing the records and previous tax returns for an activity, a tax preparer can determine whether the activity is a hobby or a for-profit activity based on these nine factors. However, taxpayers must understand that no single defining pattern or factor is conclusive and that all the facts and circumstances must be considered. If an activity is deemed a hobby, its income is reported as other income on line 21 of Form 1040, *U.S. Individual Income Tax Return*, and the related expenses are reported as miscellaneous itemized deductions on Schedule A, *Itemized Deductions*, subject to the 2%-of-AGI floor. NOTE: This deduction is no longer allowed, which leads to the question as to whether hobby deductions will be allowed against the gross income of your hobby.

Strategy #37: The IRS Wants You to Be Rich. *If you follow the rules to have a legitimate business — acting like a business, having past experience or advisors with past experience and putting in time and effort — you have a much better chance of success. And that's all the IRS is asking. That you truly work at your business.*

In a way, it does seem strange, doesn't it? It's almost like the IRS wants you to succeed. They want to help you to become rich.

Avoid Form 5213

There is some bad advice floating around the Internet that I want to dispel. Some people are suggesting you file a Form 5213 if you have a loss in your business initially. Let's explore what that really means.

The IRS provides Form 5213 for you to complete and file with them. Basically it says that you realize you have a loss in your company and that you're going to have a loss for two years. And you're asking them to not audit you for those two years.

But then, you're saying that you WILL have a profit in the 3rd year. Not only that, by filing this form you put them on notice that you have a loss.

Before you filed the form, they MAY have known about you. If you file the form, they definitely WILL know about you.

It doesn't give you a single advantage, but it does create a disadvantage.

And there's more. This is the real catch. By filing Form 5213, you are giving the IRS two more years to audit you! Normally the statute of limitations is 3 years from the filing date of your return. Filing this form extends that to 5 years.

If someone tells you to file this form because your business has a loss, think long and hard before you do this or follow other "good advice" they provide to you, for a fee of course.

The only way to prove you will have profit is by having a profit.

For a while, strictly adhering to the first three categories will be enough for your business. But at some point, you'll need to make money.

Strategy #38: Show You're a Business. *Don't file Form 5213 to tell the IRS you're going to run your business like a business. Instead SHOW the IRS you're going to run it like a business by having a successful business.*

Start a Business, But Start the Right Business

The rules about businesses and legitimate IRS-friendly businesses have not changed with the Tax Act. What has changed is the importance of having a business.

The deductions that individuals lost are mostly still available to business owners. Want your deductions back? Start a business.

Chapter 8: The Best Business to Start

The theme of this entire section is, "Start a business, if you don't already have one." You may be wondering what type of business will work for you. If that's you, then Strategies #39 – #44 may jump start some ideas for you. You don't need to have a perfect idea of what a business will be before you begin. You just need to *start*.

Or perhaps you already have a business and are looking for ways to maximize your tax savings. Make sure you check out Strategy #43 here and, of course, Section 3 is the section geared to existing businesses.

Strategy #39: Join a Multi-Level Marketing Company. *Maybe you call it an IBO (Independent Business Opportunity), a Network Marketing company, a Home-Based Business Franchise, Direct Sales Company, Seller-Assisted Marketing, Referral Marketing, Dual Marketing, Dual-Level Marketing, Concentric Marketing, Consumer Direct Marketing or Inline Marketing. There are probably even more I've missed.*

The general idea is that you are selling a product or service and if you bring other people into the company as sales people, you get a bonus or some kind of cut on their sales. Hence, the name "multi-level". You are paid at multiple levels.

There is also an evil twin to an MLM, a pyramid scheme. According to the court's conclusion in FTC vs Burnlounge, the difference between an MLM and a pyramid scheme is one of intent. Are the rewards paid out "primarily" for recruitment, or sales? Are distributors motivated by opportunity to earn rewards from recruitment, or sales of items? The following 5 factors were discussed:

Purchasing patterns -- when distributors bought premium products while non-distributors didn't, and rewards for premium products are greater, there's likely "pay to play" involved

- *Lack of value -- product value is not commensurate with rewards paid, thus motivation for purchase is to maximize rewards, thus "pay to play"*
- *Requirements to buy premium products to increase earning potential -- instead of paying reward strictly on sales amount, high reward levels are only unlocked through purchase of premium products, would indicate*

people would not have bought premium products except to unlock higher rewards, thus, "pay to play"
- *Lack of consumer safeguards -- lack of refund mechanism or rules, lack of protecting against inventory loading, etc. would indicate a possible pyramid scheme*
- *Emphasis of the Marketing -- if the marketing effort is mostly on recruitment, rather than on the products offered, it is likely a pyramid scheme.*

This doesn't mean all MLMs are bad. They aren't. And, in fact, they are often an excellent way for you to get your feet wet in the business world. You don't need to worry about finding product to sell, pricing, inventorying or fulfillment. You don't need to worry about branding, finding an office space or sophisticated accounting. All you need to do is sell. Sure, you give up some profit in this type of business, but you have also minimized your risk. That's critical as you are learning about business.

Some people go on to build businesses based solely on MLMs. Others use that experience to apply to other businesses. But, sadly, most do not have any success and
blame the model.

Earlier in this section, you saw the test that the IRS uses to determine if your MLM is a legitimate business. Remember this test doesn't say whether your MLM is legit, it says whether your approach to working in the business is legit. What is your potential for success? That's what the IRS wants to know.

I think that MLMs have gotten a bad rap because too many people have used poor marketing techniques and a few were flamboyantly illegal pyramid schemes. Not all MLMs are pyramid schemes. And not all people will succeed. But those people that learn sales and marketing skills from an MLM, often for free, taught by world class mentors, will succeed in their MLM business and subsequent businesses.

Best of all, and more on point with the tax subject of the book, is that by owning a business you're going to pick up a lot of deductions which means less tax for you.

Strategy #40: Ramp Up a Hobby*. Do you already have a hobby that could turn into a business? Do you like to do some kind of craft? There are marketplaces dedicated to selling craft projects (Etsy, for example). Maybe your hobby is rescuing dogs, riding horses, playing golf, going fishing or one of a hundred other things.*

Is there a way to ramp this up and turn it into a business? What do you do that you're passionate about now? How can this be a business? If you're stuck, I have a special invitation for you. Please go to Chapter 16 and follow the instructions to register your book. One of the bonuses you'll receive will be access to the private forum for "Taxmageddon 2018" readers.

Join us! We'll brainstorm possible ideas to turn your hobby into a business. Plus, of course, I'm around to answer questions regarding your own tax strategies to survive the tax changes. No, scratch that. You're not going to just survive the tax changes; you're going to prosper from them!

How Do You Write Off a Yacht?

A colleague of mine likes to tell the story of a wealthy client of his who came into his office with a peculiar question. The client had a successful manufacturing company in the northeast. He made a good living and enjoyed a rich lifestyle.

"How do I write off my yacht?" the client asked.

The CPA was stymied for a minute. But since the question had been a power question, one that requires an answer from most people, he thought for a bit about an answer. (Hint: Always ask: "How can I…?" Not "Can I?" "Can I" questions almost always will get you an answer of "no." It's the simple answer. On the other hand, "How can I.." requires thought. That's what it means to ask a power question.)

"Well," the CPA started, slowly. "If you had a yacht business, you could possibly have a legitimate business purpose for owning a yacht."

"OK, done," responded the client.

"Wait," the CPA said. "You need to be serious about this. You have to have a yacht business. You have to have sales, a place of business, inventory, all the things that go into having a business. This isn't just a case of buying a name. You have to really do this."

"I will," said the client.

Six months later, the client came to see his CPA.

"My new yacht business is flourishing," the client said. "I'm thinking about selling my manufacturing business."

This is a true story. The client was so involved in his hobby, now business, that his enthusiasm was contagious. He took potential customers out on his yacht to show them the benefits of the yacht owning lifestyle. And he made sales. In the end, he did sell his manufacturing business. His new business didn't even feel like a business. It was more a case of him just being able to enjoy his hobby full time.

Strategy #41: Use a Skill You Already Have. *Take a skill you already have and use it in your business. Another strategy for starting your own business is to take the skill you use in your job now and start freelancing. For example, a client of mine worked as a secretary in a Human Resources department. She began a side business helping people write impactful resumes. She'd seen a lot of resumes in her time on the job and so she had a good eye for what worked and what didn't. Make sure you don't violate any employee contracts when you freelance, however.*

Strategy #42: Online Selling. *Amazon began the FBA (fulfilled by Amazon) program and suddenly online selling will never be the same. You don't need to worry about inventory or shipping. You don't need to worry about creating a website, shopping cart or merchant service providers (so you can accept credit cards). And now with the new marketplace rules spreading across the US (starting in January 2018 with the state of Washington), Amazon is also going to collect and pay sales tax for you.*

Of course, all of that means you pay Amazon more and you have less profit, but it also takes a lot of the risk, initial capitalization and learning curve off the table.

All you need to know is how to source a product, buy it right, price it right and then market, market, market.

A lot of people move on from FBA to their own website after they get the initial details worked out. It's never been easier to start a business online.

Strategy #43: Write a blog or upload YouTube videos. *A couple of ways to make money from blogs or videos is to have affiliate links to other sites and products or use them to promote your own products or services.*

That's one strategy. Let's morph it a little bit for an additional strategy. Here's a real life story of how this strategy could work for you.

A new client of mine was going through his business and tax situation. He wanted to pay less taxes, but it looked like he had taken all of the deductions he could. (At that time, we didn't have the new Trump Tax Plan C Corporation upstreaming strategy.) I asked him where his money went. One of the biggest expenses was his wife's shoes.

She loved shoes.

She took more suitcases for her shoes than everything else combined when she traveled. And they were very nice shoes. Did I mention she loved shoes?

One idea was what if she started a blog and/or YouTube video strategy that talked about shoes? She could showcase new purchases, talk about how to wear them, when to wear them and just generally give shoe advice. At the end, provide a link to buy the shoes or other products she'd discussed and voila! She had a business with a business purpose.

That also meant she had a shoe business. Eventually, she would have to prove that it truly was an IRS-friendly business. That's where Chapter 7 comes into play.

Strategy #44: High Touch Personal Services. In today's high tech business world, the market place craves high touch personal touch. Be a massage therapist. Be a dog trainer. House sit. Pet sit. Be a personal chef for specialized diets. Do in-house gourmet dinner parties. Start a mobile pet grooming service. Diaper service. Clean-up dog poop. Dry cleaning delivery. Graffiti removal. Adventure tours. Seamstress/tailor. Mystery shopper. Mobile car wash and detailing. Professional organizer. (Please contact my husband, if you start this.) Power washing boats and RVs. Windshield repair. Business planning service. Bookkeeping. Computer repair. Photography (weddings, family portraits, pet pictures, professional pictures) Video photography of events. Drone video of events. Limo service. Food truck. Language translation. Office plant maintenance. Pool maintenance. Koi pond maintenance. Property management. Handyman services. Catering. Restaurant delivery. Window washing. Lawn mowing. Landscaping. Packing and unpacking services. Home inspection services. Home decorating. Mini-blind cleaning. Pet food and supplies home delivery. Adult day care. Personal shopper. Stylist. Make-up. Hair care services in the home.

The world has become a very busy place. People need help taking care of their lives. And, more than ever, people crave the personal touch. There is a business model here that can get you to profit quickly.

I have a home study course called "Your First Year in Business." It's a quick glance into what all it takes to get your business off on the right foot. The problem is often that there are a lot of very important questions you need to answer and actions you need to take right at the beginning. If you get it wrong, you could put your business at risk and end up costing yourself a lot in taxes. But, at the same time, you don't have time to become an expert in a lot of things. You have a business to start. In the first year, you're probably more worried about getting customers or clients than you are in figuring out how to set up your record-keeping.

It's all important, but you can't do it all. That's why that home study course is important. It distills down the actions you need to take. The next chapter covers the basics of that home study course. However, this chapter is much more condensed than the home study course.

Even if it's not your first year in business, it's good to review the basic foundation elements needed for your business. Don't just gloss over these points. If you do, sooner or later it could become very costly.

Chapter 9: Business Tax Basics Everyone Forgets

In Chapter 9, we're going to look at 8 tax basics for business owners. Most of these basics have changed as a result of the Trump Tax Plan, so if you think this is a chapter you can skip, please don't.

Tax planning has changed!

#1: Learn applicable accounting and IRS definitions.
We're not talking about definitions that you may use in your regular trade or business, but rather the definitions that the IRS or state taxing authorities use.

Retail - Retailing is the process of selling consumer goods or services directly to the customer through one or more channels of distribution for a profit.

Nexus - Nexus in this context means connection. If your business has nexus with a state under their definition, you may be required to collect and pay sales tax on eligible sales to customers in their jurisdiction, file a state income tax return and/or pay other taxes such as a gross receipts tax and/or a franchise tax.

Strategy #45: Nexus Confusion. Once you determine where you may have nexus and what kind of nexus (sales tax, income tax, other tax), determine what reporting you need to do. For example, if you have sales tax nexus in a state, look at what items you need to collect and pay sales tax on. Some states have sales tax on digital downloads. As an example, if my company had sales tax nexus in Arizona, I would be required to collect and pay sales tax on digital downloads of this book. What states do you have nexus with? The Home Study Course "Design Your Own Nexus Strategy" available at USTaxAid.com has more detailed analysis and checklists for determining where you may have nexus and what you should do about it.

The *main point of this particular Taxmageddon strategy is that you need to check out nexus for your business. If you don't collect sales tax, you'll still have to pay it. If you skip filing state income tax returns for appropriate states, you can get hammered with a lot of penalties and interest.*

The biggest mistake business owners make regarding nexus is to ignore it. That's especially true if you have an online business. You're not invisible. The IRS and/or applicable state tax authorities will find you and then the penalties will stack up quickly. The June 2018 US Supreme Court ruling in the Wayfair case has made it even more confusing for business owners. States can require that you collect and pay sales tax on goods and even sometimes on services, according to the pertinent jurisdiction's rules, even if you don't have physical presence in that state.

Service - These are trades or businesses involving the performance of services in the fields of health, law, consulting, athletics, financial or brokerage services, or where the principal asset is the reputation or skill of one or more employees or owners.

This definition became important with the Tax Cuts and Jobs Act since the pass-through entities that are service businesses and those that are non-service (product) based are treated differently for the tax reduction benefits. There is a specific exemption carved out in the act for engineering and construction companies. Under the new Tax Act, they are treated as product or non-service companies, not service companies.

Non-service - A non-service business is a business that primarily sells products or provides a service that does not meet the definition of a service business.

Strategy #46: Service vs Non-Service. *Under the new pass-through tax reduction rules, non-service businesses are treated more favorably. If you currently have a service business under this definition, can you add new cost centers in your business that sell products? If so, you may be able to shift the definition of your business from service to non-service and that can mean a lot less tax.*

#2: Verify you actually have a business.
In Chapter 7, we went through the IRS requirements for a business to be a business versus a hobby. A hobby loss is not deductible. A

business loss is deductible as long as you have active participation and sufficient basis.

Study this chapter carefully and consider making changes to make sure your business will pass the IRS tests.

Strategy #47: Don't Lose Your Loss. *If your business runs at a loss, like most businesses do in the beginning, the risk is that the IRS may decide that you have a hobby and not a business. A hobby loss is not deductible.*

It is possible to run a loss for many years and still have a true business in the eyes of the IRS. The secret is to be able to prove that you are operating in a business-like manner, getting help when you need it, putting in enough time and effort and if you don't have profit yet, you will have or you're building something of value. Don't skip this. It's okay to run a loss. Just be prepared in case the IRS questions why a business owner would want to continue running at a loss.

No Profit, No Problem
There is a little business you may have heard of before. It rarely shows a profit, but it's been publicly traded for over 20 years. In fact, the company is currently valued at $470 billion in market capitalization. The IRS has no problem believing that it's a real business and not a hobby despite it's history of having years and years of losses and very few quarters of profit.

The founder, Jeff Bezos, of Amazon knows how to paint a vision. In the past 20 years, shares have gone up 51,900%. If you invested $10,000 in the IPO, it would be worth $5.2 million today.

Don't assume that you have to always show a profit to have a business that will meet the IRS test. If you are creating something of value, that can be enough to show the IRS you're serious.

#3: Choose the right business structure.
Business structure is another big subject. Post- Tax Cuts and Job Act our strategies are different. But the good, bad and ugly of business structures are still the same. Let's start there.

First of all, let's start with the bad business structure. A bad business structure is no business structure at all. That means you don't have asset protection and you'll pay more tax.

In this case, we're talking about the Sole Proprietorship or a Schedule C business. It is possible for you form a single-member LLC (limited liability company) and be taxed as a Schedule C business. But, in this case you will have asset protection as long as it was set up properly and maintained correctly.

No Money for a Business Structure
A lawyer friend of mine told the story about someone who attended one of his business start-up seminars. During the seminar, he explained that having a business as a Sole Proprietorship without an LLC or other asset protection entity was playing with fire. Customers could sue you. Employees could sue you. Vendors could sue you. And without the right business structure in place, everything you own is at risk.

One participant stayed after the class and asked my lawyer friend about her situation. She had spent every dime she had to get a bricks and mortar boutique retail outlet started in her home city of San Francisco.

He told her that a retail outlet would get more than its share of lawsuits and cautioned her to get an LLC set up first before she opened the doors. She worried that she just didn't have the money. She needed to get the business open and make some money before she could afford to pay to set up a business entity. Surely, everything would be fine for 3 months.

About 6 weeks went by and he was surprised to hear that the fledgling business owner was on the phone. He was happy to hear from her, assuming that she had been profitable early and would be able to now get the asset protection she needed.

"Not quite," she said, when he asked if she was ready to move forward.

It turns out that someone had fallen in her store front and she was now being sued.

"What can I do now?" she asked.

"Nothing," he replied.

You have to have your business structure set up before you're sued.

Unfortunately, too many people think they'll get lucky and avoid a problem when, in fact, they can't. The lawsuit shows up too soon.

That's just one reason why the Sole Proprietorship is a bad business structure. There are actually 5 reasons.

1. You put everything you own at risk if there is a lawsuit and judgment assessed against your business.
2. You will pay an extra 15.3% self-employment tax on taxable income from the business.
3. You aren't building business credit.
4. Your Sole Prop is 6 times more likely to be audited compared to an S Corporation or C Corporation. The chances of audit go up significantly for a Sole Proprietorship if you are running at a loss.
5. NEW! If your taxable income is over the taxable income threshold ($315K for married filing jointly or $157.5K for single), you may completely lose the new flow-through tax reduction in a Sole Prop. (More on that in the next Section.)

If you form a single member LLC for your business and do not elect another tax structure, your default will be a Sole Proprietorship. If that's the case, you will have the asset protection, but you still have an issue with the other 4 potential problems.

Single Member LLC for Passive Real Estate
If you have a single member LLC for your passive real estate, it will be reported on your Schedule E. You don't have the same issues that

a business does with Schedule C. However, don't let the fact you own real estate lull you into a false sense of security.

You could still have a real estate business. The two most common forms of real estate business (not passive real estate ownership) are those that buy property simply to resell or real estate to use as short term rentals (less than a week on average) where there are significant services performed.

If you have a real estate business, you will have to report on Schedule C unless you have a business structure. That means you'll have the same 5 issues that any other Schedule C business has.

The Ugly Business Structure
The only thing worse than a bad business structure is an ugly one.

In the case of an ugly business structure, you're not only personally liable for every bad decision you might make but you are also personally liable for every bad decision your partner might make.

That type of structure is a General Partnership. Luckily, we don't see too many of those anymore. When there are 2 or more partners who own or control a business, they typically form a multi-member LLC.

Strategy #48: Fixing a General Partnership. If you have an operating business without many tangible assets inside a General Partnership, it should be fairly easy to dissolve it and form a more business-friendly structure such as an LLC. If you have appreciated assets inside the General Partnership, distributions of the property can be made at basis. So there won't be a tax consequence. Distribute assets and then contribute them into a multi-member LLC. If you are also operating a business, you can distribute out the business into a better structure like an LLC that has elected S Corporation tax status.

The key here is that a partnership can distribute out appreciated assets without a tax consequence. That gives you flexibility. If instead you had appreciated assets inside a S Corporation, the distribution would have to be done at fair market value and tax paid on the calculated gain using that fair market value, even though there was no sale.

Don't ignore a general partnership. If you have one, get out. The good news is that it won't be too hard or too expensive to do that.

We covered the bad and ugly of business structures. Now let's talk about some good business structures. They are LLCs, limited partnership (LP)s, S Corporations and C Corporations. Sometimes people want to hold their businesses inside trusts, which can work, but often not in the way you want them to work. They are audit magnets and generally set up just to provide asset protection. They do not legally provide any of the tax advantages that are sometimes touted. In fact, tax rates for trusts are much higher than they are for both individuals and for C Corporations.

Of the good ones: LLC, limited partnership, S Corp and C Corp, which is best?

Most of the time, the best business structure for a business with active, earned income (not passive) will be an S Corporation or a C Corporation.

Consider a C Corporation if some or all of the following are true:
- You want the maximum amount of tax deductions and tax savings,
- You don't require all of the income from the business to live on each month,
- You are at the highest personal tax bracket and looking for ways to reduce the tax hit,
- You intend to go public at later date,
- You generate income that will be treated as earned income, not passive income,
- You want maximum control over when and how you pay your taxes, and/or
- You want the most comprehensive medical expense deductibility available.

C Corporations aren't always the best solution if one or more of the following is true:
- It's the early days, when you don't have much or any profit,

- You're going to have losses in the early years,
- You need all the profit to live on and plan to pull it all out in salary,
- You own rental real estate or a stock portfolio and want to put it in a business structure,
- You don't want to go public, and/or
- You want to leave the business to your kids after you're gone.

Now let's talk about S Corporations. These are great when:
- The income generated will be treated as earned income, not passive,
- You're not in the highest personal tax bracket,
- You expect losses in early years,
- You want some company-paid medical insurance, but don't want or need medical expenses paid by the company, and/or
- You want to take advantage of the 20% income reduction on flow-through income.

I don't like S Corporations when:
- You have a lot of medical expenses,
- You own rental real estate or a stock portfolio you want to put in the business,
- You're in the highest tax bracket already, and/or
- You want to leave the business to your family.

And I don't like either of these structures if your business is going to hold assets that appreciate in value. Appreciating assets are better held in LLCs (limited liability companies) that have default taxation. A single member LLC with rental property, for example, is reported on Schedule E of your Form 1040. A multi-member LLC with rental property is reported on a partnership return, Form 1065.

Generally speaking, though, that while corporations are the best for active business, it's usually better to start with an LLC and elect to be taxed as an S Corporation or C Corporation. These types of structures are called LLC-Ss or LLC-Cs.

Who Can Own an S Corporation?

S Corporations are corporations that elect to pass corporate income, losses, deductions, and credits through to their shareholders for federal and state income tax purposes.

Shareholders of S corporations report the flow-through of income and losses on their personal tax returns and are assessed tax at their individual income tax rates.

To qualify for S corporation status, the corporation must meet the following requirements:
- Be a domestic corporation
- Have only allowable shareholders
- May be individuals, certain trusts, and estates and
- May not be partnerships or corporations
- Have no more than 100 shareholders
- Have only one class of stock
- Not be an ineligible corporation (i.e. certain financial institutions, insurance companies, and domestic international sales corporations).

Foreign Residents Can Now Own S Corporations

In a huge change with S Corporations and who can own them, Congress has reversed a long-standing rule. Foreign residents can now own S Corporations. However, it's not completely straightforward.

Under prior law, an electing small business trust (ESBT) could be a shareholder of an S Corporation. That part is still the same. In the past, the only eligible beneficiaries were individuals, estates and certain charitable organizations eligible to hold S Corporation stock directly. A non resident foreign individual could not be a beneficiary of an ESBT.

Under the new Tax Act, effective on Jan. 1, 2018, a nonresident foreign individual can now be as a beneficiary of an ESBT. This a huge change in tax law, likely as a response to the emerging global economy.

S Corp or C Corp?

So far there have been a lot of things to consider before you select the right business structure. And we haven't even talked about the business itself.

Businesses almost always should be held in some kind of corporate structure. That means an S Corporation or a C Corporation, or an LLC that has elected to be taxed as an S Corporation or a C Corporation (LLC-S, LLC-C).

An S Corporation is a flow-through business structure. You report the income or loss on your personal return. That means that if your income level qualifies, you get to reduce the flow-through income by 20%. The S Corporation structure is usually used for businesses in the beginning. If you have a loss, the loss can be used to offset your other income provided you have sufficient basis. You've got more flexibility with an S Corporation.

A C Corporation does not flow-through. It pays tax itself. If you personally pay tax at a high tax rate, that could be good for you. With a C Corporation, you might be able to move taxable income from your high personal tax rate to a lower C Corporation tax rate. Effective 2018, C Corporations are taxed at a flat rate of 21%.

A C Corporation also allows you take more tax-free benefits as an owner/shareholder. Not all of these benefits are available to an owner of an S Corporation.

An LLC-S is taxed the same as an S Corp. An LLC-C is taxed the same as a C Corp. For tax purposes, they are the same. There are some asset protection differences, though. A corporation will protect you if something happens with the business. An LLC will too, but it will also protect the business if there is a judgment that comes against you personally. There are a few states that have better asset protection for corporations then for LLCs (notably Colorado and Florida). For the most part, in other states, you're better off with an LLC that elects the corporate status.

Effective in 2018, there are new tax breaks for pass-through entities but if your taxable income is over the threshold, there are limitations and the formula becomes complicated. Make sure you read the next section to identify business tax strategies that will work for you.

More Good Business Structures
Another good business structure is a Limited Partnership (LP). LPs have largely been replaced by Limited Liability Companies, but there are times when I still see them used and think they make good sense:
- When you want the ownership versus the management rights and duties to be clear,
- When you want the security of a long-established entity with asset protection case law, and/or
- When you desire an optimal estate-planning vehicle that keeps control with you even where majority ownership has passed to your children, and/or
- LPs will cost more to operate safely than an LLC, and if they are real estate LPs, limited partner owners will not qualify to be real estate professionals. Limited partners are, by their legal definition, passive and non-decision-making. You can't be a passive owner AND be a real estate professional at least for that investment.

Last up are LLCs. Unless you're planning to go public; I like them best of all, for all kinds of reasons:
- They are good for holding appreciating assets that generate passive income,
- They provide beneficial tax treatment for passive income,
- They provide the simplicity and economy of operating a single structure,
- They act as an estate planning vehicle or a vehicle that allows separation between management and owners,
- They provide flexibility to distribute profits outside of the strict ownership ratio,
- They provide protection of your personal assets through state laws in many cases, and/or
- They provide the possibility to elect which business structure you want to use for tax purposes.

You may find that you need different tax strategies and structures for different times in your business life cycle. In the beginning, you're likely to have low income or possibly losses. The best business structure then is most likely an S Corporation or LLC taxed as an S Corporation.

Strategy #49: S Corporation or LLC-S? *An LLC elects how it will be taxed. An LLC that elects to be taxed as an S Corporation is commonly referred to as LLC-S. You can form a corporation and elect S Corp status. Or you can form an LLC and then elect to be taxed as an S Corporation. Generally speaking, it's better to be an LLC-S than an S Corporation. There is no tax difference. It has to do with asset protection.*

If there is a judgment that comes about because of something that happens with the business held inside an S Corporation, and the corporation has been set up and run properly with all of the required notifications, your personal assets should be safe from that judgment. The S Corporation structure will protect your personal assets from the business. But what happens if you are personally sued and there is a personal judgment against you? In that case, your personal assets will be at risk. One of those personal assets is your stock in the S Corporation. That means a successful litigant could take your stock and therefore the S Corporation.

An LLC-S will protect your personal assets like an S Corporation in most states. (There can be a problem with Colorado and Florida if you have a single member LLC. This is something you should discuss with your lawyer.) If you receive a personal lawsuit and judgment, the LLC units are safe.

That's why we generally recommend an LLC that elects corporate status instead of setting up the corporation directly and electing S Corporation status. The LLC will have better asset protection in most cases.

Set It Up Right & Maintain It
There are a lot of options online you can use to set up your business structure for little money. If you know exactly what you want, know how to draft the necessary documents and you'll be the only owner, that might be a good option.

Otherwise, we always recommend you have a legal professional help you with the set-up. If you have a partner in the venture, make sure you have clear written understanding of how you will work together, how you will handle disability, death, contributions, bankruptcy, insolvency and distributions and what kind of exit plan you have individually or together with the company. Get everything in writing right from the start. The last thing you want is to be trying to negotiate these things when the company and/or your relationship is having problems.

Once you have your professional tax strategy and have properly implemented the strategy with the right business structure(s), you may think you're done.

You're not.

Now you have to successfully maintain it. Here are some of the things you need to be prepared to do:

1. Make proper notice with others that you are operating in a business structure by signing contracts as an officer, manager or member of the structure, showing your title on business cards and other advertising and other items that the public may see.
2. Avoid commingle your personal and business funds or credit card purchases. Keep a clear trail of where the money goes.
3. Keep your business structure up-to-date according to the state requirements.
4. Hold and document shareholder or member meetings.
5. Keep detailed financial records and use proper accounting.
6. File your business tax return on time.

If you don't follow-through, you will lose both the asset protection and tax savings from your business structures.

Strategy #50: Maintain Your Entity. *The best planned business structure in the world won't help you a bit if it isn't first implemented properly and then properly maintained.*

If you're not prepared to follow the corporation (or other entity) formalities, don't even start. You could spend a lot of money to get a false sense of security. You must follow through and continue to follow through.

#4: Plan your accounting system

Most people know, at least at some level, that they need to track their income and expenses. You probably know that as well. That doesn't mean you're going to do it, but you probably know you need to do that.

What you may not know is that there are also some planning issues you should think about right up front.

Cash Basis versus Accrual Basis

Will you be a cash basis or accrual basis taxpayer? A cash basis taxpayer pays tax on income when it is received and takes a deduction for expenses when they are paid. You have more control over taxable income with a cash basis accounting system. You just don't bill out your receivables right away or rush to the bank with the checks to deposit the last week of the year to reduce your gross income. You can also reduce your net income by paying all of your expenses before the end of the year.

Or you could hold off on paying some expenses and leave them as accounts payable if you want to shuffle some deduction off to the next year. You have some flexibility.

Accrual accounting is the more accurate representation of your business profit. For tax purposes, cash basis is better.

Strategy #51: Cash Basis and Accrual Basis, Together. *One of the better strategies is to combine both accrual basis financial statements that are useful for your business and cash basis accounting for your tax return. Use a program like QuickBooks and set up your books to work with accrual accounting.*

When you make a sale, record it. If you don't have the cash yet, record it as accounts receivable offset by the appropriate income account. Then when you collect the money, the amount is removed from your accounts receivable and charged against cash.

NOTE: I say "you should" here but really I mean your bookkeeper should. Your job as an entrepreneur is to focus on sales, marketing, fulfillment, and all the million other things you have to do to keep the doors open. It's almost certain that the best use of your time isn't to be your own bookkeeper. I have a degree in accounting and lots of years in public accounting but I don't do my own bookkeeping. If you do, you get so involved in the details that you lose sight of the bigger picture. And you end up missing opportunities as well as fixing things that aren't important enough for you to be watching.

When a bill comes in, it is booked into accounts payable along with the expense item. When you pay it, the amount comes out of accounts payable and is recorded against cash.

If you set up your QuickBooks or other accounting software with accruals as explained in the previous two paragraphs, it's easy, with just the push of a button, to have the software provide the cash-basis statement you will need for tax preparation. The software can change accrual into cash for tax purposes. But the software cannot change cash into accrual for financial statement comparison and management reports. Set up your company books as accrual to get the best of both worlds.

Hybrid Accounting and Retail

If you sell products, whether they are priced at wholesale or retail or whether by internet or via a bricks and mortar store, you have to account for inventory.

When you buy or create products for resale, the items are recorded as inventory as part of your assets. It's not an expense. I'm going to say it again a couple more times simply because so many people get this wrong.

If you buy something to resell, it's inventory. An asset. It's not deductible as a cost of goods until that item is used in a sale.

If you buy $10,000 of inventory before year end and you still own it at year end, it is NOT a deductible expense. It's inventory. That's an asset not a deduction.

When you sell a product, you then remove it from your inventory account and then it is written off as a cost of goods sold deduction against the income from the sale.

There are a number of ways that people record inventory. It's best to record the purchase items as inventory when you buy them and then remove each item from the inventory when you sell the item.

At least once a year, do a physical count of your inventory to determine how much you actually have in stock. Over the year, some items may have gone missing or been damaged. Any missing items are recorded as expenses and removed from the inventory amount. Of course, you can do a physical count of your inventory more than once a year, just make sure you do a physical inventory at year end, at a minimum.

Once your business has gotten the inventory process down, the next question is probably how to derive the inventory valuation. If you have large or unique items that you sell, you probably want to track inventory by specific purchase. It is the most precise method for valuation.

However, once you make large purchases of similar products for resell, you have a number of different options available. In this case, the IRS prefers the FIFO (first in, first out) method or the LIFO (last in, first out) method.

FIFO assumes that the first unit to enter stock is the unit that will be sold, so that costs are assigned based on the oldest invoice price.

LIFO assumes that the last unit to enter stock is the first one sold, so that costs are assigned based on the last invoice price.

Strategy #52: Inventory Strategies Before Year-End. *Building inventory uses cash, but is an asset, not an expense. For that reason, buying a lot* of inventory at year-end is not a good tax saving strategy. You're better off spending money on deductible expenses.

In fact, it's better to look at liquidating some of your inventory at year end. Don't build inventory at year end, shrink it.

If some of your inventory is obsolete or damaged, write it off so that you turn some of that inventory asset into a legitimate deduction. Perhaps you could donate that obsolete inventory to a 501 (c)(3) charity so you can write off the entire amount at the value shown at on your books.

Strategy #53: Do NOT Make This Mistake with Inventory. Cash basis taxpayers sometimes reason that if they spend cash for things for their business that it will be a deductible expense. No money in the bank account = no taxable income, they reason.

This is a HUGE mistake.

Inventory is an asset. It is not an expense until the inventory is sold and it's a cost of good sold, as an expense
against the income.

If you buy up a lot of inventory at the end of the year, in a misguided attempt to reduce your taxable income, you won't have a deduction and you won't have cash to pay all the tax you'll owe. Don't make this mistake!

Capitalize or Expense?

Sometimes your business will spend money or buy items that must be capitalized and then depreciated. In this case, you won't get an immediate deduction, but have to wait to take part of the deduction each year over the depreciable life.

There are two exceptions to that. Section 179 allows you to take an immediate expense for personal property items that normally would be capitalized and depreciated.

There is also 100% bonus depreciation available in some cases. In the past, bonus depreciation was only applicable for new property that was purchased. It is now available for used property as well.

Writing Off Your Auto, Effective 2018
There are still some limitations with automobiles, but they have been relaxed. The new annual depreciation limits are:
- $10,000 for the 1st year,
- $16,000 for the 2nd year,
- $9,600 for the 3rd year, and
- $5,760 for each remaining year in the recovery period.

There is another option with bonus depreciation, but there is a catch.

You can take a deduction of $18,000 in the first year with bonus depreciation. The problem is in the second and subsequent years. In that case, you can't take a deduction in the other years until the cumulative allowed depreciation equals what you would normally have taken. In fact, that's not even so clear because it looks like you may actually not be able to take any depreciation until year 7, when you can do catch-up depreciation. For now, bonus depreciation is probably not a good idea for luxury vehicles.

If your vehicle is a 'heavy' vehicle with a GVWR of 6,000 pounds or more, you can take 100% bonus depreciation and write the entire vehicle off in the first year.

Strategy #54: Last Minute Tax Tips for Autos. *If you're concerned about taxes and you wanted to buy a new vehicle anyway, a heavy vehicle might be a good purchase for you. You don't need to pay cash. In fact, you can finance the whole thing with zero cash down. You'll still get the full deduction. However, this does not work if you lease the vehicle. And of course, this has to be a vehicle used for business in order to get the deduction.*

Repair vs Capitalization
If you have real estate rentals, the whole question of repair versus capitalization is something you'll have to deal with sooner or later. The Tax Cuts and Job Act has added a new wrinkle that has made it even more complicated.

The IRS came out with some amazingly complicated regulations in 2013, with most of the changes impacting tax returns starting in 2016. If you have an expense that extends the life of your property, you need to capitalize and depreciate that expense. If it does not, it likely is a repair.

Additionally, if a single invoice (services, products or both) is less than $2,500, it can be immediately deducted as a repair expense. It does not need to be capitalized. Note here that this is not a requirement but is a choice you can make.

Normally, we look for all the deductions you can take on your return. However, in the case of depreciation or turning a capitalized asset into an expense, there is one other thing to consider when it comes to real estate.

1. If you take the extra deduction, does it create a loss you can't offset against other income? If so, you probably shouldn't turn the capitalized expense into a repair expense or accelerate depreciation. All you will be doing is creating a suspended loss. No deduction now. And, when you sell, the depreciation has to be recaptured at a 25% flat rate. You won't have any additional tax on the repair expense, though.
2. If you hope to take advantage of the pass-through income reduction and your taxable income is over the threshold amount, you will need to rely on either 50% of wages paid or 25% of wages paid plus 2.5% of depreciable assets still being depreciated to determine how much flow-through income can be reduced. If you don't have many assets, you won't have much that is eligible for the pass-through income reduction so capitalizing and depreciating these expenses may be your best choice.

Strategy #55: Strategic Approach to Capitalization. *In the past, the strategy has usually been to take all of the write-off you can for your tax return. Now you need to consider what that will do to your eligible pass-through income reduction.*

Is it worth taking more of a write-off this year and foregoing some of the pass-through tax reduction later at tax time?

It's a question of numbers. Review your own circumstances with an experienced CPA.

#5: Do you have employees or independent contractors?

Before you jump into deciding all of your workers should be employees or they should all be independent contractors (ICs), it's important to weigh the differences. It's difficult to change an employee into an IC and if you decide one class is ICs, then later if you make an exception for one person, you could blow all of your arguments. Let's start by reviewing the seven reasons why ICs might be better for your business.

Reason #1: It's Easier to Ramp Up Your Business

You can contract with Independent Contractors (ICs) for short terms, month-to-month or just on a per-project basis. You don't have to worry about training them or providing tools for them to work. And, you should be able to get instant performance without a training curve.

The rule of thumb in a CPA firm is that it will take up to 6 months to get the cost of an employee to a break-even point. Until then, an employee is costing you money. That's why I only work with independent contractors who already have the training, education and expertise.

What about your business? How much will it cost you before an employee truly makes you money? Would an IC who can hit the ground running and who provides all their own training and tools be a better fit?

Reason #2: It's Easier to Deal with Changes

The only certainty in business is change. If a project changes, you may need to change the number and/or type of workers you have. It's much easier to cancel an Independent Contractor Agreement (ICA) than it is to let an employee go or to bring on new ones for that matter. There are fewer emotional issues and you don't have legal or benefit costs like COBRA to consider.

Reason #3: Quality Improves with an Independent Contractor

An IC who works for you will have a different mindset than an employee. He has his own business too, which means his reputation is on the line when he works with your company. He's not watching the clock and putting in the minimum effort just to collect a paycheck.

Now granted, there are plenty of clearly dedicated people in the workforce who work as employees. Your business may already have some of these wonderful employees working for you. I hope someday they get the chance to use that dedication, hard work ethic and brainpower in building their own business instead of just yours. Being an IC is usually a good deal for both the business owner and the IC.

Reason #4: Independent Contractors Are Value Focused, Employees are Time Focused

Employees are paid by the hour, the week or the month. They are not paid for a result. You simply can't pay employees the way you can pay an Independent Contractor. I think philosophically that's one of the biggest problems most businesses face.

Governmental rules and regulations require you to pay employees by "time". If they put in the time, regardless of the results, they get paid. But if you switch to Independent Contractors, you can pay based on a result. In other words, when a project completes, or when various milestones are met, or as a commission for a result.

In my tax consulting business, I have Independent Contractors who are paid for preparing tax returns. If they don't get the tax returns done, they don't get paid. It doesn't cost me a dime if they don't work, well, other than an irate client, I guess. On the other hand, if I had employees working on tax returns, I'd have to pay them by the month regardless of how many returns they completed. It's a guessing game: Who can you hire that will work hard, no matter what?

Reason #5: Lower Hidden Support Costs

When you hire ICs, you can eliminate big hidden costs. Let's say you have a business that requires someone to work on the computer during the day. If you have an employee, you are paying them for their time, plus furnishing them with a place to sit, and equipment to do their job. So you'll have additional overhead for office space, office furniture, phone/computer/equipment costs, tech support and so on. I estimate the hidden cost of an average office employee position to be about $10,400 in the first year, plus payroll taxes and benefits.

If you hire an IC, they are responsible for all of those costs.

Reason #6: Better Benefits for the Owners
As your business grows and becomes more prosperous, chances are you're going to be even more focused on looking for benefits that you can receive from the company, tax free. But in an employer/employee environment, all employees have to be treated equally. So if you put in a MERP (medical expense reimbursement plan) or a retirement account partially funded by your business, you've got to offer that same benefit package to your employees, as well. If you have many other employees, you've just picked up a huge liability. ICs do not need to be covered by benefit plans. That can be a big cost savings.

Reason #7: Less Tax
Your biggest savings with Independent Contractors will probably be payroll taxes. Payroll taxes can cost you an additional 10% or more of the salary you pay your employees. Plus, your employee is going to have to pay payroll tax as well. By switching to Independent Contractor relationships you can save yourself the payroll tax and show your new ICs how to minimize their own payroll taxes, income taxes, business taxes, and more.

Make no mistake: A properly set-up IC arrangement will mean less tax for both of you.

And now, let's look at one big reason why having an employee might be better than an IC. You may pay less taxes.

The 2018 change in how pass-through entities are taxed can depend on how much salary you pay. The limitation occurs if your business is over the taxable income threshold for the 20% flow-through income reduction. Your reduction is then limited to 50% of wages paid or 25% of wages plus 2.5% of depreciable assets. If you don't have employees and instead have ICs, the amount that will qualify for the reduction could be reduced if you have the right (or wrong) set of circumstances.

Audit Risk: Additionally, the IRS is ramping up audits of companies that have a lot of ICs. They'd rather collect the payroll taxes.

There are three main areas that the IRS will look at for determining whether you have employees or ICs. These are:
- Behavioral Control
- Financial Control
- Type of Relationship

If you have a concern about your own workers, make sure to register your book. Besides having access to a private forum where you can ask questions, you'll also be given a free audio recording on "Winning the Independent Contractor Argument."

Strategy #56: Winning the Independent Contractor (IC) Argument. Under the Tax Cuts and Job Act, having ICs might not be as important for your business. If you're not sure what is right for your business, go over the numbers. This really is an objective test, based on what will give you the best return.

If you want to make sure your workers are ICs, you will need to make sure you follow all the rules. You can't tell them how to work, when to work or where to work. And you need an IC agreement, at a minimum. The IC has control over his or her business and should have more control than you as a client.

It's not something to jump into quickly. If the IRS or the state taxing authority determines that you have misclassified workers, you'll wind up paying a lot in payroll tax, penalties and interest.

#6: Find your hidden business deductions

Your business will have two types of expenses: direct and indirect. Let's use a retail store as an example. If you buy a widget to sell, it initially goes into inventory as an asset. Then when you sell the widget, it comes out of inventory and is a direct expense against the sales income. It's better known as a cost of goods sold expense.

A direct expense occurs when you have an expense directly related to your business. If you sell a service, the cost of salary, training, payroll taxes and other expenses that occur only because of that service are your direct expenses.

You should always report your direct expenses and, for that matter, track how much profit you have after your direct expense deductions. This gives you your gross profit or gross margin. Watch the percentage (gross profit divided by the sales income) because that will be a good indicator of how your business is doing. If the gross margin suddenly goes down, you've either had an increase in costs or a decrease in sales revenue. Maybe the industry is beating you up a little or maybe you have added price pressure in your industry. Sooner or later, you're going to have to deal with it. Businesses compete based on value/innovation or on price.

I personally want to be innovative and provide services and value my clients can't get anywhere else. If price is your main concern, I am not your best solution. If overall profit is, now that's a different story.

There are other service providers who sell based on price. It all depends on what niche you pick.

Either way, you need to track your direct expenses.

Indirect expenses are items that are also known as General & Administrative. They are legitimate deductions but are more related to the overall business rather than directly related to the product or service that you are selling.

When you go looking for your hidden business deductions, you are most likely looking at personal expenses that are legally deductible. They are indirect expenses.

The IRS Code tells us that an expense needs to be ordinary and necessary to the production of income in order to be deductible. That means just about anything could be deductible, depending on your business and the way that particular expense could help you.

Don't skip over this step or wait until after the tax year is over. You will want to make sure you have clearly defined what is deductible for your business so you can get the most accurate estimate of profit for the year. This is the only way you can get the true benefit.

Strategy #57: Only Four Ways to Change Your Taxes. *YES, there really are only four ways to change the amount of taxes you pay. These are:*
- *Change the character of taxable income you have,*
- *Change the amount of your taxable income,*
- *Change your deductions, or*
- *Change the timing of your income and/or expenses*

With enough time and a willingness to change, almost anyone can pay less tax using any of these strategies.

The tried and true method is the one that takes the least amount of planning and change. Look for your hidden business deductions and change the amount of deductions you can take on your business tax return.

#7: Know your numbers.
A bookkeeper takes activities and turns them into numbers. A CFO (chief financial officer) takes numbers and turns them into activities. Your job is to understand how effective and efficient your business is working and make the changes required to maximize it.

Don't worry about being a bookkeeper. For that matter, unless you have the training, don't worry about being the CFO. You just need to have those people on your team to give you timely and accurate financial statements and reviews.

Now, your work begins. Take those analytics and work on the things that will give you the biggest return for your effort.

Use the password and link found in Chapter 16 to see a sample spreadsheet that analyzes your financial statements. Look over my shoulder as I discuss what you should do if your financials looked like this.

What is the one thing you should do now for your business? Without the proper analysis, you're just making your best guess. Maybe you're right. Maybe you're wrong. Only time will tell unless you know your numbers.

Will you be able to take the new pass-through entity income reduction? It could save you 20% or more on your taxes. It may all come down to how much your taxable income is. Wouldn't you rather find out you need to do something different while there still is time to do it? If so, then you need to have current and accurate financial statements.

Otherwise, you'll find out come tax time how much extra tax you'll pay because you were too late to implement a strategy.

#8: More than ever, year-end tax planning is critical
The Tax Cuts and Jobs Act has changed a lot of things, especially for individuals. It's a whole new way of looking at income.

If you have a business, do you have the right business structure? If you have pass-through entities, do you have an issue with exceeding thresholds? Should you add a C Corporation or change a structure to that of a C Corporation?

A pension plan can be a quick way to reduce taxable income, but it has to be set up prior to year end. Do you need to get one in place soon?

What do you plan for last minute expenditures? Is it better to deduct expenses or capitalize them? Should you accelerate depreciation or not claim it at all now?

You need to have a year-end tax planning session no later than the end of September to make sure you have time to put the strategies in place.

Section III: Strategic Business Tax Changes

Chapter 10: Pass-Through Entity Income Reduction

There are two big changes for business taxes related to business entities with the Trump Tax Plan. Pass-through entities have a possible pass-through income reduction and C Corporations have a new flat rate tax of 21%.

Those two seemingly simple changes have made a lot of differences in the strategies we use for business. Don't miss the chapters in this section! This is the good stuff.

Let's dive into the pass-through income tax changes first.

The 20% Income Reduction for Flow-Through Businesses

This new Tax Act provision is referred to as "Section 199A." Section 199A provides a 20% reduction of the income from pass-through, or flow-through, entities. This exclusion was originally just for qualified business income, but at the last minute, this definition was broadened to include pass-through passive rental income. It does not include capital gains income, however. It is just income related to a trade or business or passive real estate.

You may ask why this reduction isn't called a deduction. The answer is that I don't know. I want to use the words that the Act uses so when you hear this in another context you won't be overly confused.

That simple phrase "20% reduction of the income from pass-through entities" comes with a lot more required definitions. Let's start on those.

Qualifying Pass-Through Entities

Pass-through entities include partnerships, S Corporations, Schedule C (sole proprietorships), Schedule E (rental properties) and LLCs that are taxed as any of the above. The deduction amount is calculated on pass-through income by entity after any wages are paid to an S Corporation owner/employee or after any guaranteed payments are made to an LLC member/partner.

If you have more than one pass-through business entity, each business is treated separately. For example, if one of your pass-through entities has income of $100,000 and one has a loss of $60,000, the income from the pass-through entity would be potentially eligible for an income reduction of $20,000. The loss entity does not have to net its loss with the income from the pass-through entity.

Test #1: Income Limitation
It's tax law, which means rarely is something as simple as "you get a deduction, a credit or even a 20%
income reduction for tax purposes."

If your taxable income is under $315,000 (married filing jointly) or $157,500 (single), you get the reduction. If your taxable income is over the income limitation, there are more limitations, thresholds and rules. But for now, if you're under that taxable income threshold, you're golden.

Note that for this test, the Tax Act calls for "taxable income." A lot of people are confusing taxable income and adjusted gross income (AGI). The AGI calculation is used for determining how much of your real estate passive losses can be deducted, as well as for phase-outs of certain deductions and credits. In fact, it's used frequently in the calculation of your taxes.

On the other hand, the taxable income calculation is rarely, if ever, used. This is a first for a lot of us CPAs. You come up with taxable income by subtracting the standard deduction or itemized deductions from the AGI.

The taxable income is located near the top of the second page of your Form 1040: Individual Income Tax Return. It is your total taxable income not just income attributable to a business.

As an example, let's say you have a W-2 income job and your spouse has a successful business operating as an S Corporation.

The S Corporation is a flow-through entity and so it would seem like this new tax provision is really going to save you some money. But then you find out about the total taxable income clause. Your W-2 job pays you $200,000 per year, your spouse draws a salary of $100,000 per year from the S Corp and the S Corporation makes another $150,000 after all expenses. You just have a few itemized deductions totally $25,000.

In this example, your taxable income is $425,000 ($200,000 + $100,000 + $150,000 - $25,000). You're over the limit of $315K for married filing jointly, that means you might have lost the easy 20% reduction on the $150,000 S Corporation pass-through income. That would mean possibly forgoing a $30,000 taxable income reduction. It doesn't necessarily mean you've lost all of the income reduction for tax purposes. It just means that you're going to have to jump through some other hoops. We'll talk about that in a minute.

***Strategy #58: Get Below the Taxable Income Threshold.** The 20% Income Reduction is easy as long as your taxable income is below $315,000/$157,500. If you're a little over that and close, look for deductions. Buy a little bit of equipment you can use for the 100% bonus depreciation, buy a heavy vehicle, start a pension plan and above all else, get a good estimate of what your taxable income will be at least 3 months before year end. Plan to be below the taxable income threshold if at all possible.*

There is one other rule you need to watch. It's the qualified income limitation.

Watch Out for the Qualified Income Limitation
The 20% Section 199A reduction cannot exceed 20% of overall taxable income, excluding the reduction, less any net capital gain. If it does, then the 20% reduction is limited to the taxpayer's taxable income. Here's how it works.

Lots of Itemized Deductions Means Less Tax Reduction
Let's say you have $100,000 of qualified business income as your only source of gross income. This could happen if you have an S Corporation and don't take a salary (not recommended), have passive real estate income through a Schedule E, have a Schedule C business

or are a partner in a real estate passive company and receive a K-1.

In this example, let's further assume you have $60,000 of itemized deductions. That means your taxable income is $40,000. At first glance, it may appear that you have a tax reduction possible of $20,000 (20% of $100,000 of qualified business income). But the taxable income limitation caps your limitation to 20% of taxable income. That means you will receive a reduction of $8,000 (20% of the $40,000 taxable income).

Lots of Itemized Deductions Plus Capital Gains
Let's make this even more confusing. In this case, let's say your qualified business income is only $60,000 (instead of $100,000), you have $100,000 of capital gains and an offset of $60,000. Based on that, your taxable income is $100,000 ($60,000 + $100,000 - $60,000.) An offset is an adjustment to taxable income on the front page of Form 1040 and the standard deduction or itemized deduction total from the second page.

At first glance, it would seem that your Section 199A reduction is $12,000 (20% of $60,000 qualified business income). But the qualified income limitation says that you have to reduce the taxable income by net capital gains. That means there is actually NO tax reduction. (20% of ($100,000 taxable income - $100,000 net capital gains.)

Tax Savings but Not Self-Employment Tax
If your business is held inside a Schedule C, a general partnership where you are a general partner or most types of LLCs, you will be subject to self-employment tax on your income. That is an extra 15.3% tax on the net business income, over and above the federal and state income tax
you pay.

If you qualify for a 20% income reduction, this will apply only for the income tax calculation. The self-employment tax will still be due on the total business net income amount prior to any reduction.

This is the reason why most profitable businesses are held inside an S Corporation, a C Corporation or an LLC that is taxed as either an S Corporation or C Corporation. There is no self-employment tax for corporations.

Strategy #59 Choose the Right Business Structure. *In the past, we chose S Corporations almost always as the default tax structure for businesses and chose partnerships for real estate. Then, the LLC came along and we pretty much always chose an LLC electing to be taxed as an S Corporation (LLC-S) for businesses and the default taxation method (Schedule E for single member LLCs and Partnership for multi-member LLCs) for real estate holdings.*

Now there is another consideration due to the Tax Cuts and Jobs Act.

How will you maximize the 20% income reduction and take advantage of the new flat rate of 21% for C Corporations? The best strategy, if your income is higher than the bare minimum you need to live on, is probably to combine both an S Corporation and a C Corporation for businesses. (You can, of course, use an LLC-S and an LLC-C.) Otherwise, the LLC-S is probably still best for businesses. And for real estate, the LLC default taxation is still the best. The right business structure will protect your assets and save you on taxes. The wrong one can be very expensive.

Income from the Pass-Through Business, But Not Salary

The 20% income reduction is only for the income from the pass-through entity. The reduction can't be taken on salary from the entity. If you have a partnership, you don't take a salary, you take guaranteed payments. The same principle is true. The 20% income reduction is not available on guaranteed payments.

For example, let's say you have an S Corporation or an LLC that has elected to be taxed as an S Corporation. If your profit is $200,000, for example, and you take no salary, you may be able to take a total of $40,000 in income reduction (20% x $200,000). Not taking salary is not a good idea, though, since the IRS wants to see that you pay your fair
share of payroll taxes.

So, let's say you follow the IRS rules and pay yourself a reasonable salary. For purposes of this example, let's say this is somewhere between $50,000 and $100,000.

If you take a salary of $50,000, you will pay payroll taxes on the salary. Your pass-through income is $150,000 ($200,000 less the salary of $50,000). That means you have a possible income reduction of $30,000 (20% times $150,000), provided you otherwise qualify.

If you take a salary of $100,000, your pass-through income is $100,000 ($200,000 less the salary of $100,000). That means you have a possible income reduction of $20,000. Not only do you lose the extra $10,000 in income reduction ($30,000 versus $20,000) but you have to pay an additional $7,650 ($50,000 x 15.3%) in payroll taxes on the extra $50,000 you took in salary.

Each Business by Itself
If you have more than one business or business and real estate investments, the 20% income reduction is calculated on a case by case basis. You don't net the various pass-through businesses together. You need to calculate each pass-through separately.

Business or Real Estate Income Only
The 20% income reduction is only applicable for business income or real estate income. If you have capital gains income, for example, it does not qualify for the 20% income reduction.

What If Your Taxable Income is Over the Income Threshold?
Now let's get to the tricky part of creating the 20% income reduction strategy. What if your taxable income is over the income threshold of $315,000/$157,500?

That actually leads to another question that is going to need some additional dialog.

Do you have a service business, a product business or a blended business? Before we get there, though, and a whole new level of complexity, is there any way you can reduce your taxable income below the income threshold? Your tax life is a lot simpler if your taxable income is lower than the threshold.

Strategy #60. Year-end Planning Has Never Been So Important.
The income threshold is a cliff. If you make 1 dollar over the threshold amount ($315,000/$157,500), the amount you can deduct may disappear entirely.

Is there a chance you can get your taxable income under the threshold amount? If you make $1 million per year and need every bit of it to live on, you probably won't be able to qualify under the income threshold. If you have real estate tax losses and can take those against your income, or if you don't need all your cash to live on, maybe there are other strategies you can use.

None of that will work unless you know how much your taxable income will be for the year. Meet with your CPA by September at the latest to do your year-end planning.

Service or Non-Service Business?
Another new definition with the Tax Act is "service business." This is not the professional service business definition we have used for years with C Corporations. It's something brand new. (If you're not sure what the professional service business definition is for a C Corporation, don't worry about it for right now. It all changed with the new Tax Act so that it's not nearly as onerous.)

Under the new Tax Act, "service business" means any trade or business involved in the performance of services in the fields of health, law, accounting, actuarial science, performing arts, consulting, athletics, financial services, brokerage services (including investing and investment management, trading or dealing in securities, partnership interests or commodities) and any trade of business where the principal asset of such trade or business is the reputation or skill of one or more of its employees.

There is a notable exception for engineering and architecture. These are NOT considered services under Section 199A.

This is all a mouthful, I know, so let's break it down. Basically, if you or your employees are performing a service of any kind (except the excluded services) for a client, you have a service business. And one more comment about the excluded services before we move on, it seems that since engineering and architecture are product-based rather than service based by definition, then construction contractors and sub-contractors will be as well. Only time will tell exactly how the IRS will rule on this and other questions we're all wondering about for the new income reduction law.

Service versus non-service will become an important distinction as we move on.

Strategy #61. The Schedule C Problem. *A Schedule C business is a flow-through entity. As long as your taxable income is below the threshold, you're fine. You will get a 20% reduction on the flow-through income from your Schedule C.*

However, if your income is above the threshold, the rules get a little more complicated. If your Schedule C is a service business, you also have a second threshold of $415K (married filing jointly) or $207.5K (single). Over that, and you can't take any reduction at all for flow-through income from a service business. Between the two thresholds, the amount you can take will phase-out.

If your company is a product company, you still may qualify, but the service company business owner with taxable income between the two thresholds and the product company owner both have a limit on how much flow-through income is eligible for the pass-through reduction.

This is where the Schedule C problem occurs. The pass-through reduction when taxable income is above the threshold is limited to 50% of wages paid or 25% of wages paid plus 2.5% of depreciable assets. This is a critical point. If you have a service business with income between the two taxable income thresholds or a product business with income over the first threshold, you can ONLY take a deduction on the flow-through income up to the greater of 50% of W-2 wages paid or 25% of W-2 wages paid plus 2.5% depreciable assets.

Most Schedule C businesses don't have employees. A Schedule C owner is precluded from taking a salary. The owner instead pays self-employment tax on his or her total net income. If that owner had an S Corporation, he or she would have salary for some of the income. The salary is not subject to the flow-through income reduction but all the salaries are added to determine the basis for the limitation.

The most flexible strategy would be to use a single member LLC for your business structure if you really want to stay as a Sole Proprietorship. That way if you find at a later date you're about to lose the pass-through income reduction, you can elect S Corporation status. The S Corp election for an LLC can be made anytime for 3 years after formation under the late election rules. It's a little more difficult, but possible. The easiest way to take a late election is to elect it within the same tax year.

What About a Blended Business?

If you have a blended business (part service-based and part product-based), your business type will be determined based on the predominant characteristic.

So far, that's all the guidance we have. At some point, the IRS may require blended businesses to separate the lines of income because the rules regarding the types of businesses are different as your taxable income increases.

Strategy #62: Blend Your Business. For now, if your business is a specified service business and your taxable income is too high to qualify for the new income reduction on a pass-through entity, you may want to consider changing your business model so that you have a blended business. Even better, if your blended business is more biased toward product, you can then be considered a product business. You will save a lot more with product-based businesses under the Trump Tax Plant.

The Second Income Threshold

If you're over the threshold income amount of $315K/$157.5K, the next step is to determine if you have a service business. If you do, determine whether your taxable income will exceed the second threshold amount. That is $207,500 for single and $415,000 for married filing jointly. If so, you aren't allowed any reduction.

If you're between the first and second taxable income threshold amounts, the allowable reduction phases out. We'll talk about how the phase-out works in just a second. First, though, let's look at the wage limitations rules.

Wage Limitation Rules
First, let's start with a service business. If your taxable income is between the first and second threshold ($315K - $415K/$157.5K - $207.5), you need to use the wage threshold limitation and the amount of income reduction phases out. If your taxable income is above the second threshold and you have a service business, you do not
qualify for the 20% income reduction.

If you have a product business, you don't have a second threshold or a phase-out period. If your taxable income is above the first income threshold of $315K/157.5K, you are just subject to the wage limitation rule.

Wage limitations are the greater of (1) 50% of the W-2 wages paid with respect to the trade or business or (b) the sum of 25% of the W-2 wages paid and 2.5% of qualifying depreciable property.

The wage limitation rule applies to service businesses for taxpayers who have taxable income between the first two taxable income thresholds and to product businesses for taxpayers who have taxable income above the first taxable income threshold.

Strategy #63: Schedule C Income Reduction. If you currently have a Schedule C sole proprietorship and your taxable income is above the taxable income threshold, you won't have much for wage limitation unless you have a lot of other employees. Schedule C owners cannot pay themselves salary. One strategy if you think you'll be in that spot is to form an S Corporation or an LLC and elect S Corp tax treatment. That way you can pay yourself a salary and at least qualify for some of the 20% income reduction. (You would be able to take a reduction on income up to 50% of wages paid. Of course, there is still the limiting factor of 20% of your pass-through income and other requirements.)

There have been plenty of discussions among tax professionals regarding the second part of the wage limitation qualifier. In this case, it's 25% of W-2 wages and 2.5% of depreciable asset basis.

The definition for the 2.5% actually calls for exclusively qualified property to be used.

Qualified property for purposes of this formula means "tangible property of a character subject to depreciation" that is held by and available for use in the trade or business at the close of the taxable year. Additionally, this property must have been used in the production of qualified business income and the depreciable period has not ended before the close of the taxable year. However, the depreciable period is deemed to end no earlier than 10 years from the point at which such assets are first placed into service.

Schedule C with No Employees

Now let's say you operate a product-based company that is over the threshold for taxable income ($315K for married filing jointly or $157.5K for single). It is a Schedule C business with $100,000 of net income after depreciation. The company had purchased a piece of equipment and placed it in service. The equipment was $100,000.

With depreciation, the net income is $100,000. Because the company is over the threshold, you need to now look at the wage limitation rules. You can't draw a salary from a Schedule C, so unless you have other employees, you won't qualify for the 50% of wages limitation. Your only hope is 25% of wages (which would be zero) and 2.5% of depreciable assets (which is $100,000). When all is said and done, you are limited to $2,500 (2.5% of the $100,000 equipment) due to the
pass-through wages limitation rule.

Another solution in this case:

You could take the 100% bonus depreciation if you purchased the equipment in the current year and that would zero the pass-through income in 2018. That would help you for 2018, but not do much for 2019.

You could incorporate the business as an S Corporation. Pay yourself a salary (one-third to one-half of net income). This will give you two advantages. You'll reduce your self-employment tax and have an amount for the wage limitation calculation. Of course, you do have payroll tax on the amount you pay yourself in salary.

Calculation of the Phase-Out for Service Businesses

Now let's assume you are the sole shareholder and only employee of an S Corporation. You file a joint return with your spouse. Your taxable income is $365,000 per year, which is halfway between the first
and second threshold.

Your S Corp net income is also $365,000. In real life, it's doubtful they would be the same, but for the example, let's keep it simple.

If you pull all of the income out in the form of salary, you'll have $365,000 in W-2 income and no pass-through income. If that's the case, you won't have anything that is eligible for a pass-through reduction.

Or let's say you leave all of it in the S Corp and don't take any salary. In that case, you have to look at the wage limitation. Since your taxable income is halfway between the two limitations ($315K and $415K), you can have 50% of the amount of the normal 20% reduction at the first threshold amount. This would be calculated as:

50% x (20% x $315,000) = $31,500

Of course, in reality, you can't get away with taking zero salary from an S Corporation. You need to take a reasonable salary, per the IRS code.

Service-Based Business with High Taxable Income

In this case, let's assume you have a pass-through entity and your taxable income is over $415,000. Your taxable income is over the second threshold amount for a service-based business and so you can't take any pass-through income reduction.

No tax break for you under the current circumstances!

Product-Based S Corporation with High Taxable Income

Now let's assume you are the sole owner and employee of a product-based S Corporation that has $500,000 in profit. It's also your taxable income (just for this example.) Your overall taxable income is above the first threshold ($315K for married, filing jointly, $157,500 for single) and because you have a product-based business and not a service-based business, the second threshold doesn't matter.

Your 20% pass-through income reduction will be limited by either 50% of wages paid or 25% of wages paid and 2.5% of qualifying depreciable assets.

Based on that, let's run through 3 alternatives.

#1: You take all of the income out in the form of salary. Salary is not subject to the pass-through reduction and the income is now reduced to zero. There is no pass-through income reduction.

#2: You decide to take zero out in the form of salary. Your qualified business income is $500,000. If your taxable income was below the threshold, you would have a $100,000 reduction ($500,000 * 20%). However, your taxable income is above the threshold and so the wage limitation rules need to be considered.

You have no employees in this example and paid yourself no wages. There are no capital improvements in the business in this example. That means your wage limitation amount is zero. Your income reduction is zero.

#3: The more likely case is that you pay yourself a reasonable salary, in accordance with the IRS guidelines. Let's say that amount is $150,000.

Your pass-through net income would then be $350,000. Your initial pass-through income reduction would be $70,000 (20% of $350,000).

However, you are subject to the wage limitation. You are allowed up to 50% of wages paid, which would be $75,000

(50% x $150,000).

The total amount of $70,000 is less than the limitation, so you would have a Section 199A (pass-through income reduction) of $70,000. Not bad.

Product-Based Sole Proprietorship with High Income
Now let's assume that you have a Sole Proprietorship (Schedule C) and have no employees. Your business is a product based company and makes a net of $500,000. You are married and your taxable income is over the first threshold. We'll also assume you do not have significant capital improvements in the company.

With these assumptions, let's look at your alternatives.

Alternative #1: You can't pay yourself wages from a Sole Proprietorship. Any Section 199A income reduction would be subject to the wage limitation rule. Since there are no wages paid, there is no pass-through income reduction.

Alternative #2: Let's assume that there is actually an employee that receives $50,000 in wages. The initial Section 199A deduction would be $100,000 (20% x $500,000 in income), but under the wage limitation rules, it would be limited to just $25,000 (50% of $50,000 paid in wages.)

Alternative #3: Let's assume that you have one employee who is paid $50,000 in wages and you have a qualifying capital investment of $500,000 in equipment Your initial 199A deduction would be $100,000 (20% x $500,000) but remember, you're subject to the wage limitation rule.

In this case, you're limited to the greater of (1) 50% of wages or $25,000 (50% x $50,000) or (2) 25% of wages, $12,500 (25% x $50,000) plus 2.5% of capital improvements, $12,500 (2.5% x $500,000) for a total of $25,000. In either case, the limitation would be $25,000.

Strategy #64: Strategies with Property and Income. Reduction. Instead of capitalizing the $500,000 equipment purchase, take a Section 179 immediate expensing deduction. The sweet spot would be to take enough of a deduction to get your taxable income below the threshold. That way you don't need to worry about the wage limitation rules.

Strategy #65: Sole Prop to S Corp for Income Reduction. Form an S Corporation for the Sole Proprietorship so that you can pay yourself a salary and pass the wage limitation amount. You'll need to do a little strategizing to figure out the optimum salary. You want enough salary so that it's reasonable and that you have wages for the wage limitation rules. And you don't want too much salary so that there is no pass-through income available for the 20% income reduction.

Strategy #66: Strategies for Sole Prop and Income. Reduction. Your most powerful strategy will be to find ways to reduce your taxable income under the first income threshold, if at all possible. Otherwise, if you have a service business, change your model to have a blended business, skewing to the product side. And then make sure you can pass the wage limitation rule for at least some amount of income reduction.

Partnership Pass-Through Income Reduction

Let's say you and your partner Jennifer are in a product-based business. You are married and have taxable income above the threshold. Jennifer is also married, but her taxable income is not above
the threshold.

There are no employees in the business, which nets $500,000, or $250,000 each.

Alternative #1: Distribute $250,000 to each partner
Since Jennifer's taxable income is under the threshold, she and her husband will receive a Section 199A reduction of $50,000 (20% * $250,000).

In your case, though, your taxable income is above the threshold, so you will be subject to the wage limitation. Since your partnership doesn't pay any wages, you will not receive any Section 199A reduction.

The determination for the pass-through income reduction is done individually. Each partner's taxable income will determine how much benefit they can receive.

Alternative #2: Take out some of the income as guaranteed payments to the partners.
Guaranteed payments made to a partner count the same as wages. Let's assume that you and Jennifer both take guaranteed payments of $100,000 each. That would mean you each now have an individual pass-through income of $150,000 ($250,000 - $100,000).

In Jennifer's case, her income is still below the threshold since the change does not impact her taxable income. However, she only has a Section 199A deduction of $30,000 now (20% * $150,000). This is because her flow-through income was reduced.

In your case, you now have an amount that will qualify for the wage limitation. Your flow-through income is $150,000. Your preliminary Section 199A deduction is $30,000. Your wage limitation would be 50% of guaranteed payments (plus any wages, which is zero). The amount would be $50,000 (50% * $100,000). That means you now have $30,000 of reduction.

Guaranteed payments in this amount mean that Jennifer has less of an income reduction, but you have more of a reduction.

Multiple Pass-Through Businesses
If you have multiple businesses, the qualified business income for each is calculated separately. Your taxable income, of course, remains the same but how each business income reduction is treated will be determined on whether it is service-based or product-based and how the wage limitation, if applicable, impacts the calculation.

The Sale of Depreciable Capital Improvements
If you sell property during the year, the property will no longer be available to be used in the calculation of the 2.5% limitation. If you

buy property at the end of the year it will count toward the 2.5% limitation.

Here are some additional strategies for the new Section 199A pass-through income reduction tax break.

Strategy #67: Reduce Taxable Income. *First of all, know your taxable income. Before year end, look for every possible write-off. If you're close to the limit, you want to make sure you're under it. Just one dollar too much could mean a big difference in your tax situation.*

Strategy #68: Separate Service and Product Businesses. *For now, we are taking the position that the blended service and product business which skews to the product-based business is the best way to go. In that way, you may be able to pull the service business into the more tax-advantaged product-based business calculations. Please note that this really only matters if your taxable income is above the threshold. If your taxable income is under the threshold, it won't matter.*

Strategy #69: Match W-2 Income with Right Entities. *We don't know yet exactly what is going to happen with businesses and pass-through entities that have common paymasters. For example, let's say you have 5 real estate properties and one employee. Normally, you would pay your employee through one of the pass-through entities and then split the cost among all the properties. For purposes of the wage limitation rule, we're not sure how to divide up the W-2 wages yet. The safest bet will be to match W-2 income with the right entities. With one employee, that's difficult. But if you have more than one employee, can you divide them among the various pass-through entities?*

The pass-through income reduction adds a new complexity to tax planning. It's never been more important to be strategic before year-end so you can take advantage of this new provision.

Chapter 11: More Business Strategies and Changes

We have now gone through the most radical change from the new Tax Act as it relates to pass-through entities. It is a significant piece of this new tax law and there are strategies and situations that the Act hasn't yet addressed. We'll keep you updated at USTaxAid.com when you register your book.

In the next few chapters after this one, we'll discuss the new strategies for C Corporations due to the new flat rate tax of just 21%.

But, let's not lose sight of the fact just yet that there were other changes as well. Here are some other tax changes for businesses. These are not just for pass-through businesses, but also C Corporation businesses.

#1: Employer-sponsored retirement plan loans
The change relates to the time that you have to repay loans that you (as an employee) have taken against your employer-sponsored retirement plan.

In the past, retirement plan loans became immediately due and payable when you left your job or the retirement plan terminated. If the loan was not repaid, it would offset against other assets. In other words, it
would be a taxable distribution.

The loan could be rolled over by making an equal contribution to an IRA within 60 days of the date of the offset. In that way, you could avoid the tax. That was before the change.

Under the new tax law, you have more time to make the contribution to an IRA. Instead of 60 days, you have until the due date of your return, including extensions. This gives you more time to come up with the money so you don't have to pay tax on a distribution.

Strategy #70 Pension Plan Funding Timing. You have until the filing date of your return to fund your business pension and now, you also have until the filing date of your return to fund your IRA with the loan amount you are required to pay back. The filing date of your return is defined as the date your return is due. Without extensions, this will be March 15th for partnerships and S Corporations. If you extend, the due date will be September 15th. For individuals, your return is due April 15th but can be extended until October 15th. In general, it's almost always a better idea to extend. It will reduce your audit risk and also allow extensions of time to fund pension related contributions.

#2: Transportation Fringe Benefits

In the past, an employer could deduct the cost of certain transportation fringe benefits such as parking expenses, transit passes and vanpool costs. They were a deduction for the employer but weren't taxable to the employee.

Now, the employer deduction for qualified transportation fringe benefits is not allowed. Any payment or reimbursement to the employee for commuting costs is not allowed as a deductible expense for the employer.

There is a loophole, though. If the expense is necessary to ensure the safety of an employee, it is allowed. Also, employers can sponsor a qualified transportation plan that allows employees to have amounts withheld pre-tax from their paychecks to pay certain transportation costs.

Strategy #71: Moving Forward with Transportation Fringe Benefits. If your employees regularly work late and you provide car service, Uber or tax fare as a perk, make sure you note that this is for the employee's safety. That way you have a deductible expense.

Strategy #72: Transportation Pre-Tax Plan. If your business is in a city with expensive transportation or parking costs, you may consider setting up a transportation fringe plan that allows your employees to pay for the expenses with pre-tax dollars. It won't be a big expense for you and could be very appreciated by your employees.

#3: Bicycle Commuting Costs

Employees used to be able to deduct qualified bicycle commuting expenses, up to $20 per bicycle per month.

With the new tax Act, this commuting reimbursement is no longer deductible.

#4: Entertainment, Amusement and Recreation Provided to Employees

It used to be that an employer could fully deduct expenses for recreational, social, or similar activities as long as the recipients were primarily non-highly compensated employees. These activities did need to be directly related to the active conduct of the employer's business.

Beginning in 2018, this deduction is no longer allowed. Note that it is ONLY the entertainment expense that is no longer deductible. The meals expense is still deductible.

#5: Meals Provided to Employees

One of the little-known meals deductions previously allowed was a 100% deduction for meals, food and beverage provided to employees as long as it was provided for the benefit of the employer and at the employer's place of business.

Unfortunately, that was then. Beginning in 2018, the deductible allowance for the employer is now just 50% of the cost. It is still tax-free to the employee.

This change doesn't mean just the in-house working lunches but some get-togethers that might not be as obvious. For example, the cost for the office Christmas party is just 50% deductible now unless it meets the de minimis rules of under $25 per person.

The new 50% deduction for meals provided for the convenience of the employer on the employer's business premises goes away after December 31, 2025. It then won't be deductible at all.

#6: Housing Deduction Still Allowed

The meals expense deduction "for the convenience of the employer" was cut in half, but the housing expense provided for the convenience of the employer will still be the same. Here are some examples of how that might work.

Apartment Provided to Manager

Let's say you own a 100-unit apartment complex near a college. So you don't have to keep going back and forth to the complex, you furnish an apartment free of charge to a graduate student. In exchange, the student will keep an eye on the apartments, schedule repairs, collect rent and show apartments to prospective renters. The value of the apartment rental is tax-free to the student. Your associated costs (repairs, utilities, depreciation, mortgage interest, property taxes and the like) are all tax deductions for you.

Strategy #73: Tax-Free Housing. *If you have a child going off to school, how about buying a multi-unit residential property, putting your child in charge (likely with supervision) and taking the deduction for the costs associated with the property? When he or she graduates, you can sell or just find another student to run the property. Of course, the cost of the asset is not deductible, except for the depreciation attributable to the personal and real property. But you are building an asset and taking deductions for the other costs.*

Strategy #74: Multi-Family Wealth Building Strategy. *This strategy works for the serious real estate investor who is willing to do what it takes to grow a portfolio rapidly. Buy a multi-family unit and move into one of the units yourself. You save on rent or the cost of owning a non-income producing extra home. Use the money you save to buy the next property and move into it, or just stay where you are. The advantage is that your housing costs will be 100% deductible. The downside is that you will lose the capital gains exclusion for your primary residence when you sell. If your plan is to build, and not sell, this also may work for you!*

#7: Employee Achievement Awards

In the past, C Corporations could give employee achievement awards that weren't taxable to the employee up to the total of $400 to $1,600 depending on the type of plan.

An "employee achievement award" is an item of tangible personal property given to an employee "in recognition of either length-of-service or safety achievement and presented as part of a meaningful presentation."

Starting after Dec. 31, 2017, there is a more specific definition of "tangible personal property" provided. Tangible personal property does not include cash, cash equivalents, gifts cards, gift coupons, gift certificates (other than where the employer pre-selected or pre-approved from a limited selection) vacations, meals, lodging, tickets for theater or sporting events, stock, bonds or similar items and other non-tangible personal property.

An employee can still receive a tax-free gift certificate that allows the recipient to select tangible property from a limited range of items pre-selected by the employer.

#8: In-house Physical Fitness Deduction is Gone
Not a lot more to say here. We no longer can deduct in-house physical fitness facilities. However, the recent fringe benefit guide on the IRS site says that you can. Since these guides are not allowed as evidence in case of an audit, I recommend you just assume you can't take the deduction unless we get a formal pronouncement from the IRS.

#9: Moving Expenses for Employees
Beginning in 2018, a moving expense reimbursement is fully taxable to the employee, except for members of the Armed Forces on active duty who move pursuant to a military order.

#10: Annual Paid Family and Medical Leave
With the new law, an employer that offers at least two weeks of annual paid family and medical leave may receive a tax credit. The leave must be offered to all "qualifying" full-time employees and must provide for at least 50% of the wages normally paid to the employee. "Family and medical leave" does not include leave provided as vacation, personal leave, or other medical or sick leave.

A "qualifying employee" is an employee who has worked for the employer for at least one year, and whose compensation for the preceding year did not exceed 60% of the compensation threshold for highly compensated employees (i.e., compensation did not exceed $72,000).

The credit will be equal to 12.5% of the amount of wages paid to a qualifying employee during such employee's leave, increased by .25% for each percentage point the employee's rate of pay on leave exceeds 50% of the wages normally paid to the employee (but not to exceed 25% of the wages paid).

#11: Net Operating Losses
Under the new Tax Act, NOLs arising in tax years ending after Dec. 31, 2017, can no longer be carried back as net operating losses against prior year income for a refund. They can only be carried forward and then only used against up to 80% of the taxable income.

#12: Dividend Reduction Exclusion
Under pre-2018 law, corporations that receive dividends from other corporations were entitled to a deduction for dividends received. If the corporation owned at least 20% of the stock of another corporation, an 80% dividends received deduction was allowed. Otherwise, a 70% deduction was allowed.

With the 2018 law, the 80% of dividends received deduction is reduced to 65%, and the 70% dividends received deduction is reduced to 50%.

#13: The Domestic Production Deduction is gone
The so-called production deduction is gone. This is a deduction that was allowed for people who manufacture or re-package products within the U.S.

#14: Nondeductible Penalties and Fines
Under the new Tax Act, no deduction is allowed for any otherwise deductible amount paid or incurred, or at the direction of a government entity in relation to a violation of the law. There is an exception if the payment is identified through court order or

settlement agreement as restitution, remediation or if it is required to come into compliance.

#15: No Deduction is Allowed for Amounts Paid for Sexual Harassment that is Subject to a Non-Disclosure Agreement

A taxpayer generally is allowed a deduction for ordinary and necessary expenses paid or incurred in carrying out any trade or business.

However, a business deduction is generally not allowed for any illegal bribe, illegal kickback, or other illegal payment; certain lobbying and political expenses, any fine or similar penalty paid to a government for the violation of any law, and two-thirds of treble damage payments under the antitrust laws.

Under the new Tax Act, a tax deduction will no longer be allowed for any settlement, payout, or attorney fees related to sexual harassment or sexual abuse if such payments are subject to a non-disclosure agreement.

#16: Foreign Residents Can Now Own S Corporations

In a huge change about S Corporations and who can own them, Congress has reversed a long-standing rule. Foreign residents can now own S Corporations. However, the process is not completely straightforward.

Under prior law, an electing small business trust (ESBT) may be a shareholder of an S Corporation. That part is still the same. In the past, the only eligible beneficiaries were individuals, estates and certain charitable organizations eligible to hold S Corporation stock directly. A non resident foreign individual could not be a beneficiary of an ESBT.

Under the new Tax Act, effective on Jan. 1, 2018, a nonresident foreign individual can now be a potential current beneficiary of an ESBT. This is a huge change in tax law, likely as a response to the emerging global economy.

There is one more strategy that I'd like to talk about. The increase in standard deduction has made this an even more important strategy.

Pay Your Kids
Pay your kids for work they legitimately do for your business. In 2018, you can pay your child $12,000 and he or she will not pay tax unless they have other income. It's a deduction for your business, at a time when you may be struggling to get below the pass-through income threshold. At the very least, you'll move money from your higher tax rate to your child's 0 tax rate. If your child also puts money in an IRA, you can pay them up to $17,500 and your child still won't have to pay tax. The maximum IRA amount is $5,500 for the year.

The reason this is so much higher than in the past is because the standard deduction has increased with the new 2018 Tax Act.

Once your children are employees of your company, they can also receive paid education. This isn't the tuition reimbursement plan you might have heard of before, but rather is for training that is directly related to their employment. For example, if your child is hired to run your business's social media campaign, classes in programming, writing, English, IT and related subjects would be helpful to his or her job, the cost of these is deductible for the business.

Don't Give Investments or Business Ownership to Your Kids
First, let's look at the definition of a kid for which this is applicable.

You may have a Kiddie Tax issue if your child is:

Under the age of 18 at the end of the year, or
Under the age of 24 and is a full-time student with earned income less than one-half of their support.

In the past, the amount of unearned income (interest, dividends, capital gains, royalties and pass-through entity income) that exceeded $2,100 was subject to kiddie tax if your child was subject to the tax.

Kiddie tax was then defined as the tax rate of the parents. Under the new law, kiddie tax is the same as the much higher trust tax rates.

Unearned income that you move to minors is going to be taxed at this higher rate.

Strategy #75 Paying Your Minor Children: *As soon as possible (and is reasonable), begin paying your minor children for work that they legitimately do within your business. This will be a much better tax strategy than gifting them unearned revenue sources.*

Give Adult Dependents Part of Your Business

If you have adult dependents, such as aged parents, you now have a much reduced "child tax credit" available and no exemption deduction. If you provide over one half of the support to an adult relative, you will be eligible to receive $500 from the "child tax credit".

If your adult dependents are not reasonably able to work for your business in some way, it could make sense to give part of the business to them. This could provide a source of income to them at their lower tax rate and reduce your taxable income. Assuming that you then eventually inherit the ownership back, you would do so at a stepped-up basis.

Obviously, this is a very brief overview of what could be a complicated estate planning exercise and it's strongly recommended that you talk to an estate planning attorney and/or CPA.

Now, let's take a look at C Corporations. There were only a few changes to how they were taxed, but those changes were very powerful.

Chapter 12: C Corporations and the Tax Cuts and Jobs Act

There comes a point in almost every successful business owner or investor's life where a C Corporation may seem like a good idea. Typically, in the past, adding a C Corporation became a viable strategy when your income had reached the point where you were solidly into the top federal (and state) tax brackets. You could take some of the income from your higher taxed individual tax rate and move it over to the C Corporation.

There were two main goals with the previous C Corporation strategy. Move income from the high individual tax rate to the lowest corporate tax rate. That worked for the first $50,000 of taxable income, as long as you didn't need to pull the money right back out in the form of salary. The top personal income tax rate was 39.6% and the lowest C Corporation tax rate (for the first $50,000) was 15%. As long as you could leave the money inside the C Corporation, you just saved approximately $12,500 in federal taxes. Score!

And secondly, there were better tax-free benefits for owner/employees in a C Corporation than in any other structure.

The C Corporation made sense in the right circumstances, provided you and your tax advisor understood and planned for a couple of the trickier things that can involve C Corporations. Those things are discussed in this chapter. This has been one big change thanks to the Trump Tax Plan that will make a lot of current and future C Corporation owners very happy.

If the C Corporation made sense before, and it did, just imagine how much more you're going to love it with these new changes. But before you jump out and set up a C Corporation and commit fully and 100% exclusively to running this as your business structure, read this chapter.

There are some traps to be aware of now, just as before.

C Corporation 2018 Tax Changes

There are two big changes that have occurred for C Corporations effective for tax years that begin January 1, 2018 and after. Actually there isn't complete agreement among tax professionals on the start date for the tax changes. There is a group of notable tax experts who study tax law that believe that Congress meant to have the new tax rate applied based effective January 1, 2018 regardless of the Corporation fiscal year.

In other words, if you have a C Corporation with a year-end of June 30, 2018, the last half of the fiscal year (from January 1, 2018 – June 30, 2018) would have the new tax rate. Others say that, no, Congress meant to say that it was effective only for years beginning January 1, 2018 and beyond. I personally believe that was what was meant to be said, but like the others, I wait to see how the IRS applies the Tax Act.

It's a confusing Tax Act when you can't even get the experts to agree on when it starts!

The new C Corporation tax rate has a flat rate of 21%.

There are no longer any tax brackets. If your C Corp had taxable income of $50,000 previously, you paid 15%. Now your tax rate on that amount would be 21%. At this lowest level, it actually means more tax. However, in the past, the tax rate for the C Corporation quickly became more as you moved up the tax brackets.

We now have a flat rate. The flat rate means that as your income within the C corporation increases, the tax rate becomes a whole lot less compared to the past. The tax rate stays flat at 21%. It doesn't increase.

The second big change is that there is no longer a different tax rate for Professional Service Companies (PSC). In the past, professional services such as those offered by medical professionals, accounting, legal, architecture, engineering, actuarial and professional consulting had a higher tax rate. No longer! Now the PSC has the same flat rate of 21%.

These changes mean it might be time to review your own business structure strategy again.

Let's tackle some of the most commonly asked questions about business structures in light of the new Tax Cuts and Jobs Act.

Is it Time to Change to a C Corporation?
This is a question that we're beginning to hear a lot. Should you change to a C Corporation?

In most cases, the answer is "no." The strategy that will give you the most flexibility with your business is to add a C Corporation, not replace your current structure with a C Corporation. A word of caution before you jump into this, if the ownership of the added C Corporation is the same as your current business, any benefit program you establish for the C Corporation needs to be provided to employees of the current business. Let's look at how that would work.

Strategy #76: Dual Corporations vs Single C Corporation. *Let's say that you have a business that currently nets you $400,000. With other income and not very many deductions, you are above the $315,000/$157,500 (married, filing jointly and single) threshold. Let's assume that this is a service business in this example, so you also have the second threshold of $415,000/$207,500 (married, filing jointly and single). And we'll also assume that you have taxable income that not only puts you above the first threshold but also the second threshold. The other taxable income is not subject to payroll taxes, so we can keep the calculation clean.*

That means that you can't take advantage of the 20% income reduction. You have a service business and your taxable income puts you above the second threshold.

If you don't need every penny of that $400,000 (less taxes of course) to live, there is another option.

You can set up a C Corporation to provide some work to the S Corporation (upstream strategy) or take on a separate side income (side stream strategy) that currently is within the S Corp. More on those strategies in this chapter.

For purposes of this, let's say that you can move $150,000 to a C Corporation. That would be enough to qualify you for the 20% income reduction on all of your pass-through income. The pass-through income is now $250,000. ($400,000 - $150,000).

Your C Corporation income is $150,000. NOTE: You may also have tax-free benefits, which would further reduce the C Corporation income and reduce your tax.

You have $250,000 left in the S Corporation. You determine a reasonable salary would be $100,000. That leaves you with $150,000 of pass-through income which is eligible for the 20% reduction of $30,000 (20% of $150,000). Your taxable pass-through income would be $120,000.

In this assumption, we assumed that you would receive 40% of the pass-through income as salary. If we use that same assumption for the S Corporation pass-through income before the C Corporation, your salary would have been $160,000 (40% x $400,000)

Let's look at the savings to date:
Payroll taxes: $4,034 saved ($100,000 salary vs $160,000 salary)
Federal tax: Prior to C Corporation: $128,000 (assuming highest tax bracket of 32%)

With dual corp strategy: $52,800 (24% tax bracket x ($100,000 + $120,000) for your personal return) The tax bracket dropped because $150,000 of income came off the personal return.

$31,500 (21% x $150,000) for your corporation. Total tax is $84,300.
Federal tax savings is: $43,700

In total, your tax savings is $47,734, each and every year! Think about that. What will you do with an extra $47,734 each year?

This is why the double corporation strategy works, especially with the new tax plan in place.

If you have a business, your best business structure is almost always a corporation. That means an S Corporation or a C Corporation, or even better in most cases, an LLC that has elected to be taxed as an S Corporation or a C Corporation.

In this example, let's assume that you have a business that nets you $300,000 per year. You only need about $100,000 of that to live, consequently you're investing money as fast you can. You don't want to work forever and firmly believe that investing in real estate is a good way to provide for a good retirement.

If that sounds like you, you're an ideal candidate for the dual corporate strategy. Keep your operating company inside an S Corporation or LLC-S (LLC that has elected to be taxed as an S Corporation). This will allow you flexibility in the amount of salary you take and your distribution. As a shareholder/employee of an S Corporation, you need to pay yourself a reasonable salary. The definition of "reasonable" is what you would have to pay someone else for the work you do. As an average, it is often 1/3 – 1/2 of the net income before your salary. The rest is distribution.

If you only need $100,000 of a net $300,000 for living expenses, you can have some stay in the S Corporation and be taxed at your rate.
But that doesn't mean you need to take all of $100,000 in the form of salary. If your income in the S Corporation is $100,000, it's common to take 1/3 to 1/2 of that in salary. The rest is left as income in the company. You will pay payroll taxes on salary and if you otherwise qualify for the 20% pass-through income reduction, the rest of the income can come out in distributions, taxed at just 80% with no payroll taxes.

Or, you could instead have the rest of the income flow-through to your C Corporation. The C Corporation income is taxed at a flat rate of 21%. Assuming no employees to have to share benefits with, you may put in a benefit plan that you wouldn't otherwise qualify for with your S Corporation, but even if all you do is pay a lower tax rate, you're ahead.

The money left inside the C Corporation can then be loaned out to an investment LLC you own. You're able to invest with after tax money, that was taxed at a lower rate.

Is this the right ratio for everyone as far as what is left inside the S Corporation and what should go into the C Corporation? No, there are a couple of key factors to take into account here:

- How much do you actually need for everyday living expenses?
- Will you be under the $315K (married filing jointly)/ $157.5K (single) threshold so that your pass-through entity (S Corporation) can take advantage of the 20% income reduction?

The more money you need for everyday living expenses, the more you will need to leave inside the S Corporation (for salary and distribution). That means that this income will be reported on your personal return. If you can instead live on less, you can move more into your C Corporation. That means you will have a lower personal income, more taxed at the lower C Corporation rate and more to invest in real estate or assets.

The amount you need for living expenses is a critical factor.

Strategy #77. Use a C Corporation to Qualify for the 20% Income Reduction Benefit.

The new pass-through income reduction will mean a big savings if you can get your personal taxable income below the $157.5K (single) or $315K (married, filing jointly) threshold. One way to do that is by using the C Corporation to absorb some of your income. This only works if you can live on less than the income threshold, though. If you need to pull all of the money back out of the C Corporation, you will end up moving it right back on your personal tax return.

Those two factors should be the overriding decision-makers as you determine how much money should be in a pass-through entity versus a C Corporation.

How Do You Move Money to a C Corporation?

The next question I usually will hear from clients as we work through a dual corporate strategy is, "How do I move money to a C Corporation?"

There are two primary ways, upstreaming and side streaming.

Strategy 78: Upstreaming. *Upstreaming occurs when you have two companies. One is your operation company, usually an S Corporation. The S Corporation pays the other company, a C Corporation, for goods or services.*

If you move income from an S Corporation to another S Corporation, that won't help your tax strategy. You're moving income from one flow-through entity to another flow-through entity. It all ends up on your tax return.

If you move income from an S Corporation to a C Corporation, you reduce the flow-through income, and thus your personal income. Your C Corporation reports the income.

There needs to be a legitimate purpose for the income that is paid to the C Corporation. Maybe there is a function in your company that it is currently doing that could be moved to a C Corporation. One of my clients employed his two adult children in the C Corporation to run the marketing, management, and social media campaigns. Another client imported products from overseas in his C Corporation and inventoried them. The C Corporation then sold the products at a fair wholesale market price in the US to the client's S Corporation and to other businesses.

There are 5 steps to creating a legitimate upstreaming strategy:
1. *A legitimate service or product sale needs to be identified for the C Corporation,*
2. *Your S Corporation needs to pay a fair price for these goods and/or services,*
3. *A contract, or at a minimum a memo of understanding, needs to be written and signed,*

4. Regular invoices need to be sent by the C Corporation to the S Corporation, and
5. The S Corporation needs to pay the invoices.

If there is no net income in the C Corporation, there is no point to this tax strategy. That might mean you'll need to reduce the costs associated with the products or services provided by the C Corporation, you'll need to increase the price paid by the S Corporation, or you'll need to reduce your personal needs so that you don't need to turn around and take all of the cash out from the C Corporation.

Strategy # 79: Side Streaming. Side streaming differs from upstreaming in that instead of directly providing a product or a service to the S Corporation, the C Corporation actually takes over a separate profit center that the S Corporation might currently have. It's a separate revenue stream that otherwise would flow-through the S Corporation to your personal tax return. The upstreaming strategy is in more risk of being challenged if the amount paid is too high or the taxpayer can't show why there is truly a benefit to the S Corporation with the strategy. With side streaming, however, it's clear that this is a completely separate business. An example of side streaming might be the bookkeeping company that goes hand and hand with my tax practice. They are complementary services, but are different.

How Much Should You Pay into Your C Corp?

If you don't need every dollar of profit your company earns, you may be a great candidate for some advanced tax planning. What we're talking about here is a Retained Earnings strategy. With this strategy, you take a salary to cover your financial needs, and leave the rest (or most of it) in the C Corporation. In the right circumstances, it's an easy way to save $10,000 or more in taxes.

But to make this strategy work, you need to be able to leave part of the C Corporation's income in the business, as retained earnings.

C Corporations are the only entity that can choose whether or not to disburse the profits from the business. With S Corporations and the other flow-through structures, the IRS considers all the profit each year disbursed, and taxes you on it, even if you don't actually distribute the money.

In a C Corporation, undisbursed profits are called retained earnings.

The great thing about retained earnings is your ability to divert that money into other business investments, real estate, loans, or a pension plan, for example. In each case, you can move the money from the C Corporation to an LLC (as a loan) that make the investments or you pay yourself a salary so you can qualify for a good pension contribution.

Say you wanted to use the excess profits to invest in a real estate venture. Create a new LLC to hold the property, and then have the C Corporation make a loan to the LLC. Because the money went out of the C Corporation as a loan, it won't be considered a taxable dividend to you personally. Plus, as the LLC repays the C Corporation that money won't be considered taxable income to the C Corporation. It's simply a loan being repaid. There will be an interest expense for the LLC and that would be interest income for the C Corporation. This can be an incredibly powerful strategy for smart investors.

There is one more question to cover before we continue on with the traps of C Corporation.

How Do You Get Your Money Out of the C Corporation?
There are 3 primary ways to get money out of a C Corporation. Or at least, three that are the best known. These are:
1. Tax-free benefits,
2. Salary, and
3. Dividends

Tax-Free C Corporation Benefits
Let's start with the number one benefit that people need and a C Corporation can give you. That's your medical benefits.

Health insurance paid to an employee/owner is not deductible if paid from an S Corporation. However, it is a deduction if paid from the C Corporation.

The next health-related benefit I love is a Medical Expense Reimbursement Plan (MERP). This is a reimbursement plan, so you don't have to put money "into" a plan ahead of time, estimating how much your expenses will be. Instead your expenses are simply reimbursed by the C Corporation for a full deduction.

Using the Medical Expense Reimbursement Plan
The Medical Expense Reimbursement Plan (MERP) is commonly confused with a regular medical insurance plan, but it is actually so much more. With a MERP, you can spend a certain amount each year on medical expenses and then be reimbursed directly from your C Corporation for those expenses. The C Corporation gets a full deduction.

The annual maximum amount is set by your C Corporation. So, let's say you have a C Corporation where you and your spouse are the only employees. As long as you don't control any other companies that have employees, you can offer yourselves unlimited MERP. Every qualifying medical expense that you incur, expected or unexpected, can be reimbursed by the C Corporation and is fully deductible by the C Corporation. And, with your own plan, what you define as qualifying can be considerably broader than would be available through commercially-available healthcare plans. The MERP is better than some of the other before-tax medical plans such as HSA, MSA, cafeteria or Section 125. With these other types of plans, you have an amount withheld from every paycheck. It is then held in a fund that you can get reimbursements from. There are two disadvantages to this type of program:

1. You have to determine a year in advance how much you want withheld. Unlike the MERP, there is no way to pay for an unexpected medical cost, and

2. You are limited by law to the amount that can be withheld each year.

With a MERP though, reimbursement limits are set internally, by the C Corporation's Board of Directors.

Strategy #80: Medical Expense Reimbursement Plan (MERP). A MERP is a simple plan that you can easily set up yourself. Qualifying medical

expenses include insurance premiums, co-pays, deductibles, dental, vision, therapeutic massage, acupuncture and the like. They are 100% deductible as a business expense in a C Corporation. If you set up a MERP in your C Corporation, remember that you will need to include all other full-time employees in the C Corporation and possibly employees in any other business in which you have an interest. See "Controlled Groups" in the next chapter for more discussion on this.

Go to Http:://www.Taxmageddon2018.com/bonus/ to download a template of a MERP.

Another tax-free benefit is a company car. Your C Corporation can buy any car, and in 2018 the limits for depreciation are much higher, not to mention repairs, gas, tolls, and everything else. If you use it personally, with no business purpose whatsoever, there is a value you may need to add to your W-2. Or if you can prove business purpose for most of the time, the vehicle is considered a *de minimis* fringe benefit.

Here are some more C Corporation tax-free benefits that can also be given to owners/employees:

Achievement awards: The 2018 Tax Act clarified that tangible personal property awards for employee achievement are still deductible by an employer (except for tax-exempt organizations) and can be excluded from an employee's taxable gross income. IRS regulations in place before the tax law change restrict these tax advantages to length-of-service awards or safety awards given during "meaningful presentations." The award should "not create a significant likelihood of the payment of disguised compensation."

In addition, the IRS requires that:
- The award is a tangible item like a plaque, watch, ring or pen, or similar items, including those an employee selects from a catalog.
- The maximum excludable annual award amount per employee is $1,600, or $400 for awards that are not "qualified plan awards."

- A qualified plan award is an achievement award that is given as part of an established, written awards program and doesn't favor highly compensated employees.
- Length-of-service awards can't be received during the employee's first five years of employment or more often than every five years.
- Safety awards can't be given to more than 10 percent of eligible employees during the same year.

Employer Provided Cell Phones. The personal use of a business cell phone is now considered de minimis, which means you don't have to track personal use of your employer provided cell phone. And it's a tax-free benefit.

De minimis (low-cost) fringe benefits such as low value birthday or holiday gifts, event tickets, traditional awards (such as a retirement gift), other special occasion gifts, and coffee and soft drinks are also not income to the employee, but are deductible for the C Corporation.

Those are some of the tax-free benefits that are better with C Corporations.

You can, of course, provide other tax-free benefits such as pension plans that you can provide in other business structures.

Salary from Your C Corporation

The second way to take money from your C Corporation is by drawing a salary. If all you're doing with your C Corporation is taking money out of it in the form of salary, it hasn't helped you much. In fact, it might have actually cost you money in the form of payroll taxes you might not have had to pay if you had a received a salary and distributions from an S Corporation instead.

The salary reduces the income in the C Corporation and is reported as income on your personal return. If you need all of the money to live on, it won't leave any of the taxable income in the C Corporation to be taxed at the lower tax rate. It all goes to you and is reported on your personal tax return.

The flexibility of the dual corporation strategy will allow you to take money and pay less tax, just as long as you can leave some money in the C Corporation.

Dividends

When your C Corporation pays you a dividend, it is not a deduction for the C Corporation but it is income for you. That's where the term "double taxation" comes from. It's after tax money from the C Corporation that is taxed again when you receive it.

Those are the 3 top ways people take money out of a C Corporation. One works (tax-free benefits), one can be pointless (salary) and one costs you extra tax (dividends). There is another way, though, and it's my favorite.

Have your C Corporation loan money to an LLC you own. The LLC can then invest in real estate or paper assets. This needs to be a legitimate loan, with a signed note and
fair interest rate.

In the next chapter, we'll go into some of the traps you can run into with C Corporations that you might not expect. Avoid these traps!

Chapter 13: Avoid C Corporation Traps

Don't jump into a C Corporation without thinking through your strategy to get into the C Corporation and the strategy to get out of the C Corporation. Plus, you need strategies to get your money out of the C Corporation and avoid traps. Here are some of the most common traps you want to avoid.

The Dreaded Double Taxation Issue
Double taxation is something unique to C Corporations. It happens because C Corporations are the only business structure that pays taxes at a separate, corporate income tax rate. The other structures don't pay separate income tax. Instead,
their net profits (before tax) flow-through directly to the owners' tax returns, where those net profits are then taxed at the owners' individual tax rates. In flow-through entities, the business's profit is only taxed once.

But in C Corporations, that profit could be taxed twice. The first tax is calculated based on the Corporation's net profits (before tax). If the Corporation then pays a dividend, it is taxable to the recipient. It is not deductible to the Corporation. So the dividends are paid from after tax profits of the C Corporation and then taxed again.

In a C Corporation, you need to be aware of anything that could sound like "dividend" to the IRS. Otherwise, the IRS may classify it as a "deemed dividend." A good example occurs if you take money out of the C Corporation in the form of a personal loan. Short-term loans (those that are paid back in less than a year) are usually okay. But, if you have loans that don't get paid back quickly, the IRS can call them "deemed dividends." That means they are taxable just like a dividend. They're not deductible by the Corporation, but are taxable to you.

Another type of dividend that might surprise you is a liquidating dividend. This happens if your C Corporation shuts down without a plan. The money you take out when it ends is a liquidating dividend. It's taxable to you but not deductible for the Corporation.

Strategy #81: Avoid Paying Dividends. The easiest way to avoid double taxation on dividends is to just not pay dividends. If nothing else, take out more salary, although it's better to move the money via tax-free benefits or loans to LLCs. The liquidating dividend is the sneaky dividend. It most commonly occurs when you sell off the assets that were held in a C Corporation.

Don't put appreciating assets inside a C Corporation. These can come back to hit you with much higher taxes when you sell plus you'll get hit with a liquidating dividend tax. Avoid taking out personal loans from the C Corporation. Those can be considered deemed dividends.

Watch out for the double tax from dividends by being strategic before you pull money out of the C Corporation in a way that could be considered a dividend.

Watch Out for Controlled Group Status
The controlled group is a gotcha that has snagged some taxpayers. If you and related parties own a majority interest (50% or more) in two or more business entities.

In the past, this was a big deal if 2 or more C Corporations were owned because C Corporations had tax brackets. You lost the benefit of lower tax brackets with controlled groups. Now that C Corporations have a flat rate of 21%, it won't matter if you have $50,000 or $500,000 of profit. You still pay the same tax rate and so the elimination of brackets with controlled groups doesn't matter.

However, if you have an operating company that has employees, you may have thought about creating another entity to provide more benefits to certain employees. Look out!

You can't do that if you have a controlled group status with any other type of entity. Watch out for this if you add defined benefit plans, a medical expense reimbursement plan (MERP) or tax-deferred pension plans. It doesn't matter if another similarly owned or controlled business is not another C Corporation. You still have controlled group issues and would need to cover all qualifying employees from all other entities.

Strategy #82: Understand Controlled Group. *The Controlled Group status can happen when entities have similar interests or when one company owns another. You may actually have controlled group status between two businesses that have similar interests when the party with interests in both companies does not have control. This is a case where you need to make sure you have an experienced advisor helping you with your tax and benefit planning. The rules can be complicated.*

Staggered Fiscal Year-Ends Can Lead to Big Savings
Let me start here first. This isn't a trap. It's actually another great loophole C Corporations (and LLC-Cs) have that no other business entity does: the ability to select their own fiscal year end. All of the flow-through income structures are stuck with a December 31st fiscal year-end the same as you are.

The problem with all of your businesses closing their books on December 31st is you don't always have enough time to plan, particularly where you've got multiple business streams of income that can either be inconsistent, or tend to pay off at different times.

You could wind up with a huge pile of money that artificially inflates your overall tax rate. Or, you could find that you've done all of your year-end billings and have a big tax bill for money that isn't yet collected (if you're using accrual-based tax reporting.) Even worse, right at the exact time you may need your accountant or tax advisor's undivided attention – such as how best to structure a windfall or shortfall– they are buried under OPTR (other people's tax returns), and the answers you get are either late, incomplete or not properly thought through.

By having a C Corporation in your business mix you can often alleviate some of the pain through layering of structures. A C Corporation could be paid a management fee, or a commission of some sort, which would allow you to pull windfall money out of the S Corporation and off your personal tax bill. By selecting a different year-end date for the C Corporation, you've got a safety valve for that money. It can stay in the C Corporation until the December 31st tax-time crunch has passed, and your CPA/Tax Strategist has the time they need to best help you to manage taxes on this windfall income.

There is one warning here, though. If you have a Qualified Personal Service Corporation (PSC), you are required to use a calendar year end (December 31st).

Traps with the Qualified Personal Service Corporation

The IRS defines a qualified personal service corporation (sometimes called a QPS or a PSC) as a specific type of business where the owner/shareholder provides his or her own services for the corporation. The IRS considers most professional corporations to also be personal service corporations. In addition, the IRS has recently added actuaries, performing artists, and consulting companies, businesses that generally aren't required to be professional corporations by state professional organizations, to the list.

The Trump Tax Plan removed the distinction for tax purposes of the qualified personal service corporation. In the past, they paid tax at a higher rate. That's gone! However, a qualified PSC is still required to have a December 31st fiscal year-end, eliminating any tax-timing benefits normally available to C Corporations with staggered year-ends.

A PSC also has a lower threshold for the accumulated earnings tax. This isn't that hard to overcome, if you plan for it. Ignore it at your own peril, though! The IRS can be ruthless at accessing penalties. More on the accumulated earnings C Corporation trap and strategies to avoid a little later in this chapter.

If you think your business might be considered a qualified PSC and want to operate as a C Corporation, you have two options. You can:

- Fail the IRS qualified PSC test.
- Use strategies to deal with the PSC designation.

There are two ways to fail the test. One way is to show that less than 95 percent of all full time employees spend time in PSC activities. For example, many veterinarians also offer animal boarding and care. As long as the veterinary practice can show that its employees are spending at least five percent of their time caring for boarded pets, the practice can operate as a C Corporation without being tagged as a qualified PSC. Now the veterinary practice can enjoy all of the standard C Corporation benefits.

We see this with optometrists too. Have you ever visited your eye specialist and been able to buy your glasses, frames and contact lenses on site as well? How about a chiropractor who also sells relaxation materials, a doctor's office that sells vitamin supplements, and so on? The same theory is at work here. By offering services that are not PSC related, the owners can fail the personal service company test.

The second way to fail the test is to make sure that at least five percent of the PSC'S stock is held by persons who aren't personally providing the professional service. If you're lucky enough to be in a state that permits non-licensed spouses to also hold ownership in a professional corporation or professional LLC, this is easy. Make sure your spouse (or spouses, if there are multiple owners involved) own five percent or more.

Strategy #83: Qualified Professional Service Company. *Strategy. In the past, it was an important strategy to legally avoid the QPSC designation due to the higher tax for this type of C Corporation. That's all gone now with the new Tax Act. QPSCs will get the same low 21% flat tax. However, they will have to have calendar year ends and have a lower accumulated earnings limit ($150,000 cap instead of $250,000 for a regular C Corporation.)*

You may want to change ownership so that 5% or more is owned by people who do not work in the specialized field. Another alternative is to have a non-qualifying activity in the business. If 5% or more of all employee time is spent in that activity, you will also flunk the QPSC.

Personal Holding Company: A Possible Problem
The personal holding company (PHC) is a corporation that has been established for the main purpose of collecting dividends, interest, and other solely passive investment income. It's defined as a C Corporation that is owned by 1 to 5 individuals, who together control 50 percent or more of its stock, and 60 percent or more of its earnings are passive income.

Passive income is defined as interest, dividends, rents, and royalties, before expenses.

The problem with being classified as a PHC is the increased taxes that go along with that classification. PHC's have to pay an additional 20% on top of the regular tax of 21%.

Strategy #84: Personal Holding Company Strategies. *If you have a personal holding company (PHC), your PHC will have to pay a 20% penalty. That's on top of the income tax rate of 21%. The PHC designation and penalty kicks in if it is owned by 1 to 5 individuals, who together control 50 percent or more of its stock, and 60 percent or more of its earnings are passive income.*

Since it's not advised to hold appreciating assets inside a C Corporation, receiving the PHC designation in a corporation that does hold appreciating assets is just adding insult to injury. Appreciating assets are the ones that generate the passive income. The best way to avoid the PHC is to not put appreciating assets with passive income inside a C Corporation. They are best held within an LLC with default taxation.

If you do have passive income in the corporation, just make sure you have active business income inside that company that is more than 40% of the total gross revenue.

Strategy #85: Watch the name! *The IRS will look at the name of your company for clues to whether you fall into one of the possible C Corporation tax trap types. For example, if you say "Investments" or "Holding Company" in the name of the company, the IRS may investigate to see if you are paying tax as if you were a holding company. In another example, a taxpayer had called his business an "engineered" company. That was enough for the IRS to decide he had a Qualified*
Personal Service Company.

The easiest way to avoid these types of possible IRS problems is to make sure the name of your company doesn't imply something different about your business.

The Accumulated Earnings (or Retained Earnings) Trap

When a C Corporation has accumulated $250,000 in retained earnings, there can be a penalty assessed. If you have a Qualified PSC, the accumulated retained earnings cap is just $150,000. This is a tax the federal government set up to make sure that C Corporations distribute profits from time to time.

The government's view goes something like this:

1. The more retained earnings a company has, the more attractive it becomes to investors.

2. The more attractive the investment is to investors, the longer an investor will want to hang onto it.

3. The longer an investment is held static, the lower the tax revenue. Remember, the government doesn't collect any tax until the stock gets sold and the investor pays the tax on the selling price less the basis plus sales costs.

The government determined that by installing a tax on retained earnings, sooner or later, a C Corporation would rather make distributions (dividends) to investors so they could avoid having the C Corporation face a penalty. If the penalty was high enough, the government reasoned, at some point even the largest investors wouldn't be able to persuade a C Corporation to not distribute profits. And once those profits were distributed, the government could collect tax on the profits received by the investors.

A great example of this is Microsoft. By 2004, Microsoft had retained earnings of approximately $60 billion and was paying dividends of around $0.16 per share each year. Investors were wondering if they would ever get some serious money out of the business, short of selling their shares. That year, Microsoft made a one-time dividend payout to its shareholders of about $32 billion, along with doubling its annual dividend rate to $0.32 per share.

Why had Microsoft held out so long? There are many reasons, but one of the most commonly-cited ones was that Bill Gates had held up the dividend payout because of the impact it would have on his taxes. Because of his position as a major shareholder, Mr. Gates had the clout to persuade the directors to hold off on paying out distributions. When they were paid out, Bill Gates received some $3.6 billion and donated the entire amount to charity, offsetting the tax hit he would otherwise have faced on such a huge windfall.

Strategy #86: Excess Accumulated Earnings. *If your retained earnings are above $250,000 (or $150,000 if you have a qualified personal service company), you could face a 20% additional tax. The easiest way to avoid that is to pay a dividend. It's easy, but not practical if you want to avoid double taxation.*

Another, preferred way to avoid this penalty, is to prove that you are retaining money for reasonable business needs. Some examples of those reasonable needs are:

Planed expansion of facilities and activities,
Acquisitions of related businesses,
Loans to customers and suppliers,
Reserves needed to meet competition,
Contingent liabilities, and
Working capital needs to weather up and down cycles.

Keep good records of the needs, even including them in your annual minutes for the business. The IRS rule says you must have a "specific, definite and feasible" plan in order to justify this way out of the penalty tax.

You do not need to submit anything to the IRS directly. But in an audit, they will ask for proof that you had a reason for the accumulation of retained earnings. I recommend to my clients that they include something about that in the annual minutes for the corporation.

Trick: Using a C Corporation in a Low (or No) State-Tax State

Earlier in the book, I talked about a tax strategy using a C Corporation and an S Corporation together, known as a dual corporation strategy. This strategy works great in states like Nevada, Texas and Wyoming, which have no state personal or corporate income tax.

However, it's not quite as simple as you might hope, or been told by someone who is trying to sell you a Nevada,
Texas or Wyoming corporation.

Don't rely on a salesperson to give you the straight scoop on this. This is something you definitely want to think through first with your tax advisor.

You need to have a reason for using a state other than your home state, and that needs to be more than, "I want to lower my taxes." Setting up a C Corporation in another state just for this purpose could run afoul of the economic substance law. This says that you have to show why you have the C Corporation set up in another state.

It's not enough to prove you don't have a connection in your home state for tax purposes, you have to also prove you do have a connection to the tax-free state that has economic purpose.

Strategy #87 *Prove Economic Substance. The Tax Courts have allowed taxpayers to have legal tax avoidance as a reason for engaging in a transaction, even to the point of setting up another Corporation. However, there must also be some kind of other economic purpose. In this case, though, you would be trying to change the state nexus. The federal government will be less interested than your home state will be.*

California is notorious for trying to bring corporations formed and operating outside the state into its state. If 25% or more of business is generated by California residents and businesses, then California views this as a non-resident business with California tax liability.

In general, you want to show that you have some kind of tie to the tax-free state by having employees or independent contractors in that state. Go to http:://www.Taxmageddon2018.com/bonus/ to see more specific cases by state.

Trap: Holding Appreciating Assets in a C Corporation

In general, you never want to have appreciating assets such as real estate held within a C Corporation. To demonstrate why, let's go through an example of holding property inside an LLC (limited liability company) versus a C Corporation.

Let's say you and your partner buy a property for $600,000. Over time, the property appreciates to $2,000,000 and you sell the property.

In an LLC that is being taxed as a partnership: You have gain of $1,400,000 that will be reported for you and your partner. In my example, you and your partner have equal shares, so that means the $700,000 each is taxed as long-term capital gains.

Assuming you and your partner are paying at the top long-term capital gains rate of 20%, the tax per partner would be: $140,000. This also assumes no depreciation recapture and that neither of you are subject to alternative minimum tax (AMT). We'll just keep it simple.

Total tax when held in an LLC: $280,000

In a C Corporation: You have a gain of $1,400,000 that is taxed at the flat C Corporate tax rate of 21%. The tax per partner is technically nothing, because it's all taxed at the C Corporation rate. The total tax for the corporation is $294,000.

But it doesn't stop there. All the money is still held within the C Corporation. How are you going to get it out? If you take it out as dividends, it'll be taxed again.

The dividend tax, at the highest rate of 20%, would be a total of $280,000 on $1,400,000 paid to you and your partner.

Total tax if the appreciating property is held inside a C Corporation: $574,000.

Even if you decide to not distribute out the money in a form of a dividend, the IRS may consider that the C Corporation has a liquidating dividend (and tax it like a dividend) if there is no remaining purpose for your C Corporation.

The moral of the story is: Do NOT put appreciating assets inside a C Corporation.

But what if it's too late? What if you already have appreciating assets inside a C Corporation.

Strategy #88 Fixing Appreciated Assets Inside a C Corporation.
Occasionally, I'm asked about how to fix the fact that appreciated assets are being held inside a C Corporation. There really are only three options:

1. *Sell the asset, pay the tax on the gain and the tax on the dividends.*
2. *Sell the asset, mitigate the gain with as many expenses as possible and draw out salaries so they are deductible (or the extent to which it is reasonable).*
3. *Elect S Corporation status and wait 5 years. If you sell within that 5 year wait period, you have to pay built in gains tax which effectively means you are taxed as if you still were a C Corporation.*

The best strategy, of course, is to not be in the position. But if you are, these are a few options to consider.

What doesn't work: Don't just distribute out the asset with the idea you can sell it personally or through a better entity. When you distribute out an asset from an S Corporation or a C Corporation, it is taxed as if you sold it. That's even worse than paying tax on the projected fair market gain of a sale. In this case, you pay tax on gain for something you didn't even sell!

Should You Have a C Corporation?
Hopefully, after you've gone through all of this information you have the only right answer for the question: Should I have a C Corporation? And that answer is: IT DEPENDS.

A C Corporation can be a wonderful tool, if it meets your needs. If it's not the right fit, it can be cumbersome and expensive to run. Here are a few more strategies until we move into the final part about traps (and unexpected benefits) of C Corporations.

Strategy #89: Double Taxation Issue. *Don't just assume you can avoid double taxation from dividends by never paying dividends. You may be subject to a deemed dividend, which occurs when you take a personal loan from a C Corporation that you don't pay back right away.*

It's better to loan the money from the C Corporation to an LLC and from that do your investing. However, don't make this a sham transaction. If you need that money to live on, then take it out in salary. It's a deduction for the corporation and income for you.

Strategy #90 How Do You Take Money Out of Your C Corporation? *There are two questions you need to answer before you start any C Corporation. First, how will you get your money out of your company? And secondly, how will you exit the company?*

There are three good ways to take money out of the C Corporation and 2 ways that don't work well.

For the good ways:

Salary. This is a deduction for the C Corporation and income for you.
Tax-free Benefits. These are deductions for the C Corporation and not income for you. This is probably the best of all worlds.

Loan to an entity for investment. It's not a deduction for the Corporation, but it's also not income for the LLC. Make sure you have good documentation and pay, or at least accrue, interest.

For the bad ways:

Paying a dividend. This results in double taxation.
Taking a personal loan. This could be considered a deemed dividend and also will result in double taxation.

Don't start a C Corporation until you also know how you are going to exit the Corporation. What is the end game? With a C Corporation, it's not as simple as closing down an S Corporation or an LLC. The C Corporation is a separately taxed entity, different from a flow-through entity.

Your C Corporation End Game

If your business end game is to make a public offering, then a C Corporation is your best solution. It is possible to start in another entity that you then roll into your C Corporation. There are many steps to that and you'll need both a good lawyer and CPA on your team
before you do that.

If you're starting a smaller C Corporation, one that will be closely held, then most likely the end game is a gift or sale to family or employees. If that's the case, you may want to explore some of the options for pre-funding that eventual sale in a way that gets you some tax breaks.

For example, a popular way to fund an employee purchase is with an Employee Stock Option Plan (ESOP). Rather than selling the business to a single employee, an ESOP allows you to transfer ownership of the business to all qualified employees.

ESOPs are usually treated as a workforce benefit. Employees receive an ownership stake in the business as part of their compensation, with shares that are held in trust until each employee leaves the company.

When an ESOP is used to fund a sale, the employee invests cash in the ESOP trust, which is then used to acquire the owner's shares in the business over time. In some cases, the ESOP can be funded through commercial financing, reducing the amount of time it takes for the seller to receive proceeds from the sale.

More commonly, ESOPs are funded through seller financing. Essentially, the ESOP acquires all of the owner's shares at once and pays the seller for the shares with a note that yields a healthy interest rate. Ownership of the company transfers to the employees and the seller receives the sales price plus interest.

As a seller, an ESOP can be a convenient way to achieve multiple sale goals, provided you can afford to finance a significant portion of the sale price. Also, an ESOP may provide important tax advantages (e.g., deferral of capital gains tax), depending on how the transaction is structured.

If you plan to just sell to one or more buyers in a strictly cash sale, then the question is, "How will you get your money out?" Let's look at what happens to the money in a standard sale of assets within a C Corporation.

Once the corporation's assets have been sold off and all the financial obligations have been met, any remaining cash can be distributed to the shareholders. This is typically done according to shareholders' ownership in the company.

For example, if there was $150,000 left over, and you owned 60 percent of the company's stock, then you would get $90,000 (60% x $150,000). These disbursements can be adjusted if shareholders have claimed other assets of the company. Say you claimed a company-owned truck that was worth $20,000. That value might then be added to the "pie" that gets divided among the shareholders. You'd get 60 percent of the combined total of $170,000. That's $102,000 -- your $20,000 truck plus $82,000 in cash.

The other shareholders would receive a greater share of the cash.

For tax purposes, the IRS treats a corporate dissolution the same as a stock sale. Shareholders are selling all their stock for whatever amount they get from the corporation.

If the amount a shareholder receives exceeds his stock basis, then the difference is a taxable capital gain. If the shareholder gets back less than his basis, then he has a capital loss he can use to reduce his tax liability. There are tax effects for the firm, too, since C corporations pay taxes. If the corporation distributes an amount greater than shareholders' basis in their stock, then the corporation reports a loss on its final tax return. If it distributes an amount smaller than the shareholders' basis, then it reports a taxable gain. In other words, a shareholder's gain is the firm's loss; a shareholder's loss is the firm's gain.

There is a lot to consider when you're planning your C Corporation's end game.

Strategy #91: Smart Exit Plan for a C Corporation. *Don't start a C Corporation unless you also have a plan on how you will exit the C Corporation. What's your end game? If you're planning to sell, and it will be an asset sale, you're looking at a lot more taxes. So, the better plan if you start a business you plan to sell assets from is to operate as a flow-through entity. Most of the time, the S Corporation is the better solution.*

Now let's look at one of the C Corporation benefits that can be most important, if you're in the right set of circumstances.

Other C Corporation Benefits
If you have a tech start-up, or any other kind of big idea that is going to require venture financing, you'll probably need to have a C Corporation. If you are going to take private equity funds and institutional funds as investors, they'll want a C Corporation as well. Basically, if you're going big, you're going that way as a C Corporation.

Investors often do not want to be a part of the annual accounting of the company and don't want to deal with unknown and unexpected tax obligations from a pass-through entity. Instead, they are simply looking for the opportunity to buy stock and liquidate it at an appreciated price.

There are some special C Corporation advantages that you'll want to put in place, if it fits.

Qualified Small Business Stock (QSBS) must be stock in a domestic C Corp. If the stock is held for 5 years, then the stockholders will receive a tax free sale up to $10 million or 10 times the investment made to purchase that stock, whichever is greater. Tax free!

Additionally, Internal Revenue Code (IRC) Section 1045 provides a mechanism to roll over gain of disposed stock into a new similar investment (similar to a 1031 exchange).

Another benefit that applies to C Corp stock is IRC Section 1244, which allows an ordinary loss deduction for up to $50,000 (or $100,000 for married couples filing jointly) on losses from the disposition of qualifying stock. You won't be subject to the normal limitation of $3,000 per year of capital losses.

A final reminder about C Corporations. Unless you are planning to go public or have another business purpose for a C Corporation, the reason you're probably considering one is to save on taxes. If that's the case for you, the only way it works is if you can leave some money inside the C Corporation as income. The money isn't lost. It is just safeguarded for investments, by loaning to an LLC. However, if you need every dime in order to pay your personal expenses, this won't work for you.

Strategy #92: A C Corp doesn't work unless the money can stay in the company. *If all you are doing is taking the money back out from the C Corporation for living expenses, you're defeating your tax strategy. Where does your money go? Is there a way to turn your expenses into tax deductions? If that's so, then you may be able to free up cash that you can leave inside the C Corporation. Otherwise, a C Corp strategy just won't work.*

The $500K per Year Poor House

As a CPA tax strategist, I have the opportunity to work with people from all walks of life. We only work with business owners (or people who are serious about wanting to be business owners) and/or real estate investors (or people who are serious about wanting to invest in real estate.) There are a lot of ways to have a business or investments and I've learned things from all of the people I meet in my practice.

I'm going to make this story actually a composite of real life stories. This is actually a cautionary tale, but on the outside, and to most people, it seems like a success story.

Dr J was a very successful doctor with a successful niche. He worked very hard and was on call practically 24/7. He and his partner had a business, but the "partnership" was more the case of them simply sharing an office space and some support staff. They each made money only when they worked. There were no other cost centers that provided additional income.

Dr. J didn't want to always keep working like that, but he had no money left to invest. "Everything," he said "goes to taxes. I need a change!"

We had just a few months until year end, so we didn't have a lot of time to develop a strategy. One thing that stood out was that he had not used any type of business structure strategy. For example, his wife did not work outside the home. Maybe she could supplement their income (and more importantly, legal deductions) by taking on a function in the business like marketing, back office support, social media management or something she liked.

In the end, there was nothing she was interested in doing, so we had to find another solution.

There was one more opportunity. Dr J had been asked to provide some articles for a scholarly magazine about his practice and how he was so successful with his income. He would be paid for that. Plus, it would provide some marketing for his and his partner's medical practice.

His partner agreed to pay an amount to another corporation that Dr J may set up. Plus, Dr J would get paid by the publications. But there was one caveat regarding the payment from the medical practice. The payment had to come from Dr J's share of income. So, in all likelihood, the income was simply money that would have come to him anyway.

He wrote the articles. He got paid the money by the publications but it wasn't as much as he had thought. Still there was an opportunity for some tax savings because the money would be paid by the medical practice that was in a pass-through entity to a C Corporation. This was pre-2018, so C Corporation income was taxed based on brackets. The first $50,000 of taxable income was taxed at 15% so Dr J didn't have to pay the tax at his 39.6% personal tax rate. He would save approximately $12,500 in federal taxes.

The problem is that he needed every penny of money that he earned through the PC. Whether it came to him in the form of salary or distributions, he needed that money every month.

He took out a loan for $50,000 to use personally so that he could transfer $50,000 of income to the C Corporation. Honestly, I wasn't a fan of that strategy because he now had interest to pay on the loan and that whittled away at the tax savings he received. He also invested in some no down payment rental properties as a way to create passive income. The problem is that the rent didn't cover the expenses. "No problem," he said. "At least I'll get the write off."

I had to then explain that his $500,000 adjusted gross income (mainly from his medical practice) meant that he couldn't take passive real estate losses against his other income. Once your income is over $150,000, you cannot use any passive real estate losses to offset earned income unless you or your spouse (if married, filing jointly) qualify as a real estate professional

There is a 3 part test for the real estate professional status: (1) Spend 750 or more hours in qualifying real estate activities and spend more time in real estate activities than any other trade or business, (2) Materially participate in the real estate property, and (3) Each property must individually qualify unless you make a valid aggregation election.

We didn't get past the first qualification. His wife did not want to be a real estate professional.

Between his high home mortgage, property tax bills, insurance, HOA dues, utility bills, landscaper, housekeeper, cost for the private school for his two children, two expensive car payments and other accoutrements of the "good life", he barely had enough money left over at the end of the month to put anything in savings. Now, with the real estate, he actually was negative every month. He was borrowing just to stay afloat.

So even though our strategy would have saved him, at minimum $12,500 per year, he didn't have a cent to spare to put it in place.

Now, in 2018, the savings in this example would be even greater because the C Corporation tax rate has dropped from a high of 35% to a flat rate of just 21%. But he will actually be paying even more in taxes because he won't get to deduct all of the itemized deductions he's taken in the past. This was mainly due to the limitation on the deduction of state and local taxes plus property taxes to just $10,000 per year. His property taxes alone are more than that.

Because his taxable income exceeded the second threshold for his service business (medical practice), he didn't receive any tax cuts.

And now he couldn't even fund an IRA.

He will pay even more in taxes. He will have even less for his future. He's on a treadmill that is just going faster and faster.

The best strategy in the world doesn't mean anything if you aren't willing to do things differently. You have to properly implement the strategy. You have to follow through even if it means changes you don't want to make.

These changes might mean starting a business. It might mean cutting back on personal expenses so you can invest for your future. It might mean learning what a good investment really is and doing some more due diligence before you jump into a deal.

Taxmageddon means change. For some people, change is opportunity. For others, change is destruction.

Where will you be a year from now?

Chapter 14: Real Estate Investor Changes in Tax Cuts & Jobs Act

If you have real estate investments, this chapter is for you. One of the tax benefits of owning real estate is depreciation. First, let's recap how depreciation is different from other real estate deductions. Next, we'll look at some of the strategies prior to the 2018 Tax Act. And, then, of course, we're going to look at new strategies designed to take advantage of the big changes in tax law.

Three Types of Deductions

For tax purposes, there are three types of real estate expenses:
> Direct Expenses,
> Indirect Expenses, and
> Phantom Expenses.

Direct Expenses

A direct expense is an expense that is directly related to the property. It would include mortgage interest, property tax, repairs and other expenses that wouldn't exist if you didn't have this rental property.

With the exception of repair vs improvement strategies, you should always report all of your direct expenses. (For more information about these types of strategies, please make sure you register your book at http://www.Taxmageddon2018.com/Bonus/. The keyword to get it registered is located in Chapter 16.) This is true even if the direct expenses push you into a loss that ends up being suspended.

A suspended loss is better than no loss. Report all of your direct expenses.

Indirect Expenses

Your indirect expenses are legitimate expenses that are deductible but aren't directly attributable to a property. Some examples of indirect expenses could be:

> Accounting
> Cell phone charges

Computer
ISP
Software, and
Travel.

Just like with direct expenses, always report all your available indirect expenses, even if you can't currently take the deduction against your other income. At the very least, these deductions will create a loss that will be suspended and be of benefit to you later. It's not ideal right now, but if you don't report them now you quite possibly will lose these deductions completely.

The one possible challenge with indirect expenses will be with expenses that really can't be reasonably linked to an active real estate business. For example, sometimes I meet people who have spent thousands, even tens of thousands of dollars, on real estate coaching or mentorship. Is it deductible?

Maybe.

If you pay for education to get you ready for a new trade or business, the cost is not deductible. If you already have a trade or business, education may be deductible. In that case, you need to prove that you really are in business already and that the education is going to help you in that business.

Let's say you have several properties and you attend a class on landlord law to help you know what tenant rights are. You've got a deductible expense.

However, if you haven't bought a property yet and you attend classes to learn how to find properties, how to find tenants, how to manage real estate and a dozen other things, you probably don't have a deduction.
You must be in business first.

A client of mine faced an IRS challenge when he took expensive personal development classes and attempted to deduct the cost against his real estate properties.

Unfortunately, he met me too late.

He reported the classes too early or started the business too late. Either way, if he had a business started when he took the classes, he would have had the deduction.

The IRS caught on and challenged him. And, he decided to handle initial meetings himself. He made some statements to the auditor that were later used against him. This was a case more of audit strategy (or lack thereof) then whether there was a legitimate expense or not. Most of the time, courses in personal development are considered a deduction against a legitimate business provided it can be shown that this will make you a better leader or manager for your business.

Once you have a legitimate real estate investment business, make sure you deduct all of your indirect business expenses. Do this even if it creates a loss you can't currently deduct on your return.

Phantom Expense

Depreciation, a phantom expense, is different. That's because in the case of direct or indirect expenses, it's a use it or lose it situation in the current year. If you can't take advantage of the loss in the current year, you can carry it forward until there is passive income to offset it or you sell the property. But if you don't report direct or indirect expenses in the current year, you can't "catch them up" in subsequent years. You may be able to amend a previous tax return, but that costs your money, time and increases your audit risk. And you have a limited time in which you can amend returns.

In the case of the deprecation phantom expense, you can catch up past depreciation. You can ignore it. You can accelerate it. It's available when you need it. And that's why, out of the 3 types of real estate expenses, depreciation is the only one with which you can be strategic.

Deductibility of Real Estate Losses

We discussed suspended losses and the fact that you can't always deduct your real estate losses in the year they occurred. Now let's take a step back and discuss how and when you are able to deduct real estate losses. And, more importantly, when you cannot take those deductions.

If your adjusted gross income (AGI) is under $100,000, you can take up to $25,000 of real estate losses against your other income as long as you have active participation and basis. You actively participated in a rental real estate activity if you (and your spouse) owned at least 10% of the rental property and you made management decisions or arranged for others to provide services (such as repairs) in a significant and *bona fide* sense.

Management decisions that may count as active participation include approving new tenants, deciding on rental terms, approving expenditures, and other similar decisions. If you are married, you must file as married filing jointly in order to take advantage of the real estate professional status or in order to take "up to $25,000" of real estate passive loss against income when eligible and your AGI is less than $100K.

A time share does not qualify for the real estate loss deduction ever and neither does ownership in a limited partnership when you are only a limited partner.

If your adjusted gross income is over $150,000, you cannot take any deduction unless you or your spouse qualifies as a real estate professional. The real estate professional (REP) status can be a little complicated. That's why there is an entire Home Study Course devoted to this topic at USTaxAid.com.

If your adjusted gross income is between $100,000 and $150,000, the amount you can deduct phases out.

Allowed or Allowable Depreciation
Before we move on to the rest of the depreciation strategies, I want to address a lingering myth about depreciation.

The IRS code actually says that when you sell your property, you must recapture depreciation that is allowed or allowable. That one phrase "allowed or allowable" has created all kinds of heartburn for CPAs over the years. The reading of the code made it seem that if you didn't take a depreciation deduction, then the IRS was going to force you to recapture depreciation you could have taken, even if you didn't.

The IRS set that all straight in 2004, over 10 years ago.

The IRS issued Rev. Proc. 2004-11 which permits a taxpayer to make this change even after the disposition of the depreciable property.

Revenue Procedure 2004-11 allows a taxpayer to change the taxpayer's method of determining depreciation for a depreciable or amortizable asset after its disposition if the taxpayer did not take into account any depreciation allowance, or did take into account some depreciation but less than the depreciation allowable, for the asset in computing taxable income in the year of disposition or in prior taxable years. Because the taxpayer is permitted to claim the allowable depreciation not taken into account for this asset, the taxpayer's lifetime income is not permanently affected by the "allowed or allowable" rule.

In other words, Rev. Proc. 2004-11 allows the taxpayer to deduct the unclaimed depreciation even after disposition. With this, the IRS effectively did away with the "allowable" depreciation rule. As a result, a taxpayer who has claimed less than the depreciation allowable for its property will no longer risk permanently losing an allowable depreciation deduction.

Bottom line, if anyone tells you must take a depreciation deduction because of an allowed or allowable depreciation rule, just tell them they are over 10 years late to the party.

Skip Depreciation

If you cannot deduct your real estate loss against other income, then you want to minimize your real estate loss. Always deduct your direct expenses and your indirect expenses. If you have a loss, stop. Do not take a deduction for depreciation.

Let's say you have more than one real estate investment property. Use the aggregated net income or loss for determining whether you have a loss.

If you have income, your ideal situation would be to take just enough depreciation to zero out the income amount. If you are able to take losses against your other income, you may want to be a little more strategic with how much depreciation you take.

Catch Up Depreciation
You are allowed to catch up depreciation if you have missed a few years or if you perform a cost segregation study.

This is a time when you want to make sure you have a good strategy. Don't catch up depreciation in a year in which you cannot take the real estate deduction.

Cost Segregation Study
A real estate property is generally comprised of 3 components: land, personal property and real property. Land is not depreciable. Real property (the building shell) is depreciated over 27.5 years for residential property and 39 years for non-residential property. Most of the time all the personal property is also lumped together with the real property value and the total is then depreciated over 27.5 or 39 years.

Another option is to perform a cost segregation study. There are companies that can do that for you, starting at about $5,000 for each property. If you have some real estate, construction or like experience and can follow a template, you can also perform your own cost segregation study. It's generally not recommended that you personally prepare your own cost segregation study on a large commercial project, but you can certainly do that for single family or small multi-family homes.

The cost segregation study will assign values for the personal property. The lives for the various elements will be between 5 years and 18 years. Since these lives are shorter than the standard 27.5 or 39 years, there is faster depreciation.

After you've done the cost segregation study, you can either just begin with the new lives or you can catch-up depreciation. This is all part of your strategic use of the depreciation deduction with your real estate.

Prior to the 2018 Act, the biggest question was "How much real estate loss can you deduct?"

The 2018 Act has added a few new wrinkles that must be considered before you move forward with your depreciation strategy.

100% Bonus Depreciation on Real Estate

Effective with the purchase of new or used property made after September 27, 2017, you can take 100% bonus depreciation right away provided the property had been put into service already. The bonus depreciation is not allowed on property that was part of the original purchase. In other words, if you buy a new property, you can't allocate part of the purchase price to personal property you then use the 100% bonus depreciation on. Instead, this must be used on property you buy after the original purchase.

The property has to have already been put in service prior to making improvements in order to get the benefit of 100% bonus depreciation for improvements.

Strategy #93: Put Your Property in Service First. *If you buy a real estate property and start immediately remodeling, you are a real estate developer. That means there are no deductions until it's put in service. Meanwhile, the remodeling expenses are capitalized to be depreciated or amortized later. You can't depreciate the depreciable property and you can't take the 100% bonus depreciation.*

The strategy here is to immediately put the property in service. It could mean that you start off renting the property for a low amount and not for the eventual purpose. For example, let's say you buy a property that is a low end single family home and you want to remodel it to a luxurious standard. First rent it at the low end, and then improve it. One of my clients bought a blank lot and wanted to find a way to take some write-offs on it. After our consultation, he put up perimeter fencing and rented the space to a nearby contractor who needed a spot to park some of his construction equipment.

Both of these strategies put the property in service. Don't just inventory your property. Put it in service first!

In order to take the bonus depreciation, the subject item has to have been purchased later and is in a depreciation class that is 20 years or less. For example, landscaping is depreciated over a shorter period. That means it would be 100% deductible. So would paving on a parking lot or concrete for a driveway.

Make sure you fully read the rest of this chapter, though. There can be a downside to the 100% depreciation and you need to be ready with a strategy for that.

Section 179 Deduction for Non-Residential Real Estate

A Section 179 deduction allows you to immediately expense purchases. Right now, with the 100% bonus depreciation, it's been less necessary. However, it is one more option. The Section 179 expense deduction is only available for non-residential real estate.

In the past, the Section 179 deduction was more useful because only new property qualified for bonus depreciation of any type. That has changed now. Both used and new property qualify for both Section 179 expensing and 100% bonus depreciation. The only real difference is that you can use 100% bonus depreciation but can not use the 179 deduction for residential real estate.

Pass-Through Tax Reduction Concerns

One of the biggest changes with the new Tax Act is the way that pass-through entities are taxed. There is a 20% flow-through income reduction available under certain circumstances. Since real estate investments almost always are held in some kind of pass-through structure, this is definitely an important benefit to take advantage of.

First, if your taxable income is under $315,000 (married, filing jointly) or $157,500 (single), you can skip the next part. Your net flow-through income will get the 20% flow-through income reduction.

If your income is over the threshold, then you still may qualify for at least part of the reduction. The amount of net income that is subject to the reduction is limitation to the greater of 50% of W-2 wages paid or 25% of W-2 wages paid + 2.5% of qualified depreciable assets. The qualified depreciable assets are assets that are still being depreciated.

Now you see the problem with immediately expensing or depreciating assets. It's a trade-off between getting the reduction now and in the future or immediately expensing or depreciating the asset to reduce your income to qualify for the flow-through income reduction.

Strategy #94: Wait on Taking Bonus Depreciation or a Section 179 Deduction. *Let's say that you can't deduct real estate losses against other income. In that case, taking the bonus depreciation probably won't make sense. Additional losses just mean more suspended losses. If instead, you wait to deduct the asset by using the slower depreciation or maybe even avoiding depreciation entirely, you have the asset still sitting there for the day in which you can take a bigger deduction by using depreciation and catch-up depreciation.*

There really isn't anything new about bonus depreciation or Section 179 for non-residential rental properties. The same strategies apply. For sure, if you don't get a deduction against your ordinary income, don't accelerate the write-off. Prior to the 2018 Tax Cuts and Jobs Act, we were concerned about suspended losses. Now you need to be concerned about both suspended losses plus the potential loss of some of the tax reduction which you would get from the 20% flow-through income reduction.

There were a lot of terms used in this chapter that might be new to you or you may have questions about. Cost segregation study, bonus depreciation, Section 179, real estate professional status and more are just a few of them. If you have questions on any of this or other real estate and business tax strategies, make sure you register your book at http://www.Taxmageddon2018.com/Bonus . Hint: Go to Chapter 16 to find the password you'll need to join the private forum only for *Taxmageddon 2018* readers.

New Rules on Rehabilitation Tax Credit Amount

The new Tax Act repealed the 10% tax credit for qualified rehabilitation expenditures for a pre-1936 buildings. The credit for qualified rehabilitation expenditures for certified historic structures has been increased from 10% to 20% effective January 1, 2018.

There is a transition rule if you have owned a pre-1936 or historic property prior to January 1, 2018 and are undergoing rehabilitation now (or plan to soon).

Strategy #95: Real Estate Tax Credits. *The ADA tax credits are still around (50% of eligible access expenditures up to $10,250 per year.) When you're looking at rehabbing a historic property for commercial use, you can double up the 50% ADA credit with the 20% historic tax credit. Remember that tax credits are used directly against your taxes. It is not just a deduction. Tax credits are a lot more powerful!*

What You Need to Do NOW

The important thing is to plan ahead. By September of the taxable year, you need to have an estimate of your pass-through entity income and your total taxable income. That's the only way you'll have enough time to do something before it's too late.

So far you've learned about the new law, read real life success tax saving stories, cautionary tales and strategies.

None of it means a thing. You have to do two more things, implement the strategies and then properly report them. It's all up to you. What will you do with this information? If you're ready to take charge of your wealth building, cash flow accelerating future by putting the Trump Tax Plan to work for you, make sure you follow the steps in Section 4. This is meant to be used as a workbook. Get a pen and paper and get to work! Your bank account will thank you.

Section 4: Put Your Plan in Action

Chapter 15: What Will You Do Now?

We have covered a great deal in *Taxmageddon*. Many of the old standard tax strategies simply don't work anymore. If you are going to take the "wait and see" approach, you will see that it's actually a "wait and pay" plan. If you do nothing to prepare for Trump's Tax Plan, you're going to pay a whole lot more in taxes.

It's not that it's a plan for the rich as much as it is a plan for those who will take action and probably change a few things about how they make money and pay expenses.

There is one more point to make. This isn't meant to be a book you put on the shelf. This is a dynamic piece of law. It will be changing and evolving for years. The only way to stay current on the law and to make sure your plan is right for you is to stay involved and informed. In Chapter 16, you'll find the information you need to register your book. Once you unlock that vault containing thousands of dollars worth of special reports and audio broadcasts, you'll find there is actually quite a bit you can do to control your financial future.

What You Need to Do NOW
The important thing is to plan ahead. By September of the taxable year, you need to have an estimate of your pass-through entity income and your total taxable income. That's the only way you'll have enough time to make any required changes before it's too late.

There are 4 ways we can help you take control of your taxes:
1. Become a year-round tax client. We approach tax planning differently at my firm, US TaxAid Services. Our CPAs work virtually with clients, so you work with someone whose experience matches your goals, not simply someone who is closer geographically but doesn't have the experience you need. We work year-round, so there is ongoing strategy and implementation. No bad tax surprises!
2. Schedule a personal tax consultation with me. The number of consultations is limited each month, with the quota usually

selling out by the end of the first week. Check it out at http://www.ustaxaid.com/consultation/
3. Join the twice monthly live coaching sessions. I'll take questions during the session and there is a complete Home Study Course valued at $99 - $249 included with each session. The sessions are recorded so you can review the information again. Check it out at https://www.ustaxaid.com/coaching-program/
4. Register this book! Go to Chapter 16 for information on how to register this book and join our exclusive forum ONLY available for *Taxmageddon 2018* readers.

So far you've learned about the new law, read real life success tax saving stories, cautionary tales and strategies.

None of it means a thing. You have to do two more things: implement the strategies and then properly report them to the IRS and state tax agencies.

It's all up to you. What will you do with this information? If you're ready to take charge of your wealth building, cash flow accelerating future by putting the Trump Tax Plan to work for you. This chapter and the corresponding information at http://www.Taxmageddon2018.com/bonus/ is meant to be used as a workbook. Get a pen and paper and get to work! Your bank account will thank you.

Please download the "Taxmageddon Review" pages as part of the Insider Secrets section of the bonus information. Then, follow along as we review the chapters and look for your most important take-aways from each chapter. This is a way to help you avoid getting lost in all the data.

Chapter 1: The Standard Deduction versus Itemizing

Summary: Most Americans will soon just use the standard deduction, instead of itemizing their deductions. How will the changes impact you? Take a look at the Chapter and the strategies again. With that information, complete these questions below.

What Are the Key Points for You?

What Questions Do You Have?

What Strategies Do You Want to Implement Right Now?

What is the Most Important Thing You Need to Do Right Now? Your "one thing" could be finding a new tax advisor, cleaning up your bookkeeping, starting a business, getting serious about a business, starting a charity or simply finding out how much the Tax Cuts and Jobs Act is going to help you. Or, you could have something entirely different that you need to do.

Chapter 2: Losing the Miscellaneous Deduction

Summary: The miscellaneous deduction is gone from the itemized deductions. Not everyone used these on their tax return, but for those that did, this could be a very expensive change.

What Are Your Key Points?

What Questions Do You Have?

What Strategies Do You Want to Implement Right Now?

What is the Most Important Thing You Need to Do Right Now? If this particular chapter wasn't as relevant to you because you don't currently report miscellaneous deductions as part of the itemized deductions, it still may have triggered an item for your "to do" list. Or maybe you simply want to add one thing that you were prompted to do after reading another chapter. When you have finished this part of the workbook, you will have 14 "one thing I must do items". From that, you'll have additional exercises. Don't lose the opportunity to rank the importance of one of the things that you currently are thinking about. Add something to every chapter in the "What is the most important thing you need to do right now?" section

Chapter 3: Strategies for Your Personal Residence

Summary: The tax deductibility of your house has changed. The old "get a better job, buy a bigger house" strategy doesn't work anymore. Or at least, if it does for you, you're going to have to work that much harder because you don't get the same tax breaks. Does that change your own plan with your primary residence?

What Are Your Key Points?

What Questions Do You Have?

What Strategies Do You Want to Implement Right Now?

What is the Most Important Thing You Need to Do Right Now?

Chapter 4: Dependent Deductions

Summary: You no longer receive exemptions for your dependents. And, the standard deduction has been increased. Those two factors alone may change your strategy for deducting payments to, and on behalf, of your family. There also is a little tidbit about how 529 plans have changed along with a strategy to get a little back from most states. Maybe your home state is one of them.

What Are Your Key Points?

What Questions Do You Have?

What Strategies Do You Want to Implement Right Now?

What is the Most Important Thing You Need to Do Right Now?

Chapter 5: Individual & Investment Tax Strategies for 2018 & Beyond

Summary: Quite simply, tax strategies and wealth-building strategies based on tax leverage, have changed. Individual taxpayers who don't have a business and/or real estate investments will have a harder time breaking out of their current level. Paper assets were never great for tax strategies and they just lost any advantage they had. Crypto currency has an array of confusing tax laws, which all mean more taxes than you're probably expecting. This is an important chapter for those who are counting on a job and paper assets.

What Are Your Key Points?

What Questions Do You Have?

What Strategies Do You Want to Implement Right Now?

What is the Most Important Thing You Need to Do Right Now?

Chapter 6: Why Start a Business?
Summary: A business has always been the best way to get a tax deduction. Post-Trump Tax Plan, it's pretty much the only way for most people. Why have a business? What does it take to deduct a business taxable loss against other income? How do you legally create a tax loss while you are putting money in your pocket? This whole section is key to making a change in wealth-building.

What Are Your Key Points?

What Questions Do You Have?

What Strategies Do You Want to Implement Right Now?

What is the Most Important Thing You Need to Do Right Now?

Chapter 7: Sure You Think You Have a Business, But Does the IRS Agree?
Summary: If your business has a loss for consecutive years, generally 3 years in a row, you may have an issue with the IRS claiming that you have a hobby not a business. If you have a hobby, instead of a business, the IRS will not let you take the loss against your other income. Of course, if there is income, you have to pay tax on the

income, no matter what. The IRS has tests designed to see if you have a business or a hobby.

What Are Your Key Points?

What Questions Do You Have?

What Strategies Do You Want to Implement Right Now?

What is the Most Important Thing You Need to Do Right Now?

Chapter 8: The Best Business to Start
Summary: It's never been easier to start a business. You can start an online business overnight. You can have a retail store without the storefront or employees. Or, if you want to go high touch instead of high tech, there are literally dozens of ideas.

What Are Your Key Points?

What Questions Do You Have?

What Strategies Do You Want to Implement Right Now?

What is the Most Important Thing You Need to Do Right Now?

Chapter 9: Business Tax Basics Everyone Forgets
Summary: Nexus confusion, new tax definitions from the Tax Cuts and Jobs Act, entity strategies, inventory, last minute tax strategies, independent contractors and the annual expense or capitalize question, there is a lot to consider in this chapter. In fact, this chapter may be the one that you want to read again completely before you finish this part of the workbook.

What Are Your Key Points?

What Questions Do You Have?

What Strategies Do You Want to Implement Right Now?

What is the Most Important Thing You Need to Do Right Now?

Chapter 10: Pass-Through Entity Income Reduction
Summary: By far, one of the most complicated parts of the 2018 Tax Act are the rules regarding pass-through entities. If your taxable income is below the first threshold ($315,000/$157,500), it's easier as long as you understand what kind of income can get the income reduction and your overall reduction is over the alternative income calculation. Once you're over the threshold, the way you can take the income reduction and even if you can get one at all, will depend on whether you have a service or a product business. There are a lot of strategies in this chapter to help you maximize your benefit from this complicated law.

What Are Your Key Points?

What Questions Do You Have?

What Strategies Do You Want to Implement Right Now?

What is the Most Important Thing You Need to Do Right Now?

Chapter 11: More Business Strategies and Changes
Summary: It's easy to get lost with all of the strategies available for pass-through entities and C Corporations. There were actually a number of changes to fringe benefit deductions, which created even more new strategies. Here they are.

What Are Your Key Points?

What Questions Do You Have?

What Strategies Do You Want to Implement Right Now?

What is the Most Important Thing You Need to Do Right Now?

Chapter 12: C Corporations and the Tax Cuts and Jobs Act
Summary: There were two major changes for C Corporations, 21% flat rate and change in how Qualified PSCs are taxed. Those two changes have created a whole lot of new strategies.

What Are Your Key Points?

What Questions Do You Have?

What Strategies Do You Want to Implement Right Now?

What is the Most Important Thing You Need to Do Right Now?

Chapter 13: Avoid C Corporation Traps
Summary: The C Corporation provides great benefits and some potential traps like double taxation, controlled group status, personal holding company excess tax and accumulated earnings penalty, among others. Are you ready for the potential risks, as well as the benefits, of a C Corporation?

What Are Your Key Points?

What Questions Do You Have?

What Strategies Do You Want to Implement Right Now?

What is the Most Important Thing You Need to Do Right Now?

Chapter 14: Real Estate Investor Changes in Tax Cuts and Jobs Act
Summary: The 20% income reduction for pass-through entities may impact real estate holdings, provided they have income. It can't be used as a reduction for capital gains tax. Plus, there are some changes to tax credits for real estate developers and big depreciation changes.

What Are Your Key Points?

What Questions Do You Have?

What Strategies Do You Want to Implement Right Now?

What is the Most Important Thing You Need to Do Right Now?

Next Step
At this point, you should have a lot of data and be engaged again with the material.

If you have questions on the book or your situation that you don't mind sharing in an open group, please post in the Insider's Only forum. That is available at your special page once you register your book.

What strategies do you want to implement? My guess is that you have at least 20 or more strategies right now. If you're like me, you'll have a lot more.

In this next exercise, please use the downloaded form again and while considering those strategies, refine them to the following:

In the next 90 days, I will:

Make these top 5 contacts:

Learn these 3 new capabilities:

Let go of these 5 things:

Start these 5 new projects:

Contacts
The 5 contacts you need could be related to finding a new CPA, finding a bookkeeper, hiring a lawyer or even something related to

operating your business. You could already know this person but you want to change up the relationship so you can use them more in your business and investments. Maybe you need an advisor, a new client, a software guy or an insurance advisor. We don't operate in a vacuum. The people around us will encourage and inspire us, or stop our future progress. That choice is up to you. If you want to make a change, this is a good
place to start.

This is your next 90 day focused plan. It's up to you to use it, or not. I recommend you continue to do this exercise every 90 days to keep on track. It's what works for me.

Capabilities

A capability is something that makes you better at what you do or want to do.

What does your business or investments need for you to do? Do you need to bring in more clients? Do you need to streamline fulfillment? Do you need to know how to interpret your financial statements? If your plan is to build your real estate portfolio, do you need to keep a good journal so you can keep your deductions or real estate professional status?

Examples of these 3 new capabilities could be learning more about some aspect of tax law, software or something that will help you work more efficiently in your businesses and investments. Maybe it's a new skill or simply learning to let go and delegate. Maybe it's time to learn how to create systems that work so you don't have to work. If you think about it, you'll know what that needs to be.

Letting Go

For everything you add to your "to do" list, there is something you need to add to your "don't do" list. Before you start piling on the list of things you want to accomplish in the next 90 days, please think about what you want to let go of doing.

Maybe you're ready to let go of doing your own bookkeeping or doing your own filing.

We're automating a function that currently takes 3 people to do and never seems to work smoothly. I personally am not letting go of a thing, but my teammates are. Look at your current systems, is there something you're doing that a better system would eliminate. Technology can do a lot. Is there something you could let go of right now and turn over to a well written system? Maybe outsource some of your duties.

What 5 things do you want to let go of during the next 90 days?

Start These 5 New Things
Now finally, it's time to do the list of things you want to accomplish. What 5 things do you want to do in the next 90 days?

This is a rudimentary start to beginning an ongoing 90 day plan. Work ON your business, not just IN your business. Make more money by focusing on what you do best. And then, of course, make a plan to save on your taxes by putting the new strategies in place that you've learned about in this book.

Chapter 16: The Last Inch

Now listen to the rule of the last inch. The realm of the last inch. The job is almost finished, the goal almost attained, everything possible seems to have been achieved, every difficulty overcome — and yet the quality is just not there. The work needs more finish, perhaps further research. In that moment of weariness and self-satisfaction, the temptation is greatest to give up, not to strive for the peak of quality.

That's the realm of the last inch — here, the work is very, very complex, but it's also particularly valuable because it's done with the most perfect means. The rule of the last inch is simply this — "Not to leave it undone. And not to put it off — because otherwise your mind loses touch with that realm. And not to mind how much time you spend on it, because the aim is not to finish the job quickly, but to reach perfection." – Alexander Solzhenitsyn

The best strategies in the world, don't mean a thing if you don't put them in place.

That's implementation. And then once they are in place, you need to properly report them on your tax return. That's compliance.

Throughout *Taxmageddon 2018*, you learned a number of strategies. Which ones will you use to put your plan in place?

To review the strategies with me on an audio, please go to http://www.Taxmageddon2018.com/bonus/ to register your book.

The password when you register is **LessTaxNow**

Every book has a lot of detail behind it. You can't put it all in a book. Some of it is video, some of it is audio and some of the additional pieces are checklists and "how to" add-ons that need to be added as supplemental parts.

If you don't act upon the information, it's just that, information. When you put these strategies in place, you can get amazing results. But nothing changes without implementation.

Here's what one of our clients discovered when he put just a few of the strategies in this book in place.

Creating a Whole New Life
Alec was an impressive man. He'd been dealt a tough hand, but refused to let his physical challenges get him down. His legs were paralyzed and he was confined to a wheelchair. He wasn't going to get better, but the good news was that he wasn't going to get worse either.

He had gotten Social Security disability and had medical insurance paid by the government. But it was more like survival living. The amount he got was just subsistence. He lived with his sister and her husband. He had no way of getting around. He relied on them for everything.

Disability income can be a trap. If he started making money, he would lose the disability payment. And once lost, it was very hard to get it back. Most people in this predicament get stuck there. But Alec decided to make a break out of the trap.

He started learning about selling through Amazon's FBA (Fulfilled By Amazon) program. He realized that he wouldn't be able to find the sources for products, inventory or ship products. So he concentrated on learning what he could do – market. He learned about ranking for the products he had, writing copy, getting good reviews and making sure he could make the sales. He found the products, vetted drop shippers and started with an inventory at Amazon.

He concentrated on what he could do, and left the rest to experts. He started making money. Within the first 18 months of his business he had grossed $120,000 and netted $50,000. His disability income was gone, but that didn't matter anymore.

And that's when he came to talk to our firm. The first thing I wanted to do was put him into an S Corporation, or actually an LLC that elected to be taxed as an S Corporation. This would save him 15.3% on the net income from the business, or approximately $5,800. That represents the self-employment tax. With an S Corporation, there are costs, though. And like any smart business move, you need to look at both the cost and the benefit.

An S Corporation with income is required to pay the owner a salary. A general rule of thumb is 50% of the net income must be paid in salary. The Social Security and Medicare tax on that salary is a total of 15.3%. So, in essence, you save ½ of the $5,800, or $2,900. There will be an initial set-up fee for the S Corporation. And you'll have to file one more tax return and probably pay someone to help you with the payroll reports. If you can get the payroll set up yourself, QuickBooks has a good program to help you file your payroll returns. You're still required to file them, though. And if your bookkeeping is simple you may be able to do it yourself on QuickBooks. Again, you need to be diligent and current on your bookkeeping. If you won't do it, be honest up front and save yourself a lot of heartache.

For Alec, his total cost to set up was about $500. The set-up is a one-time fee. The federal and state return preparation was $550 per year. He did his own bookkeeping and filed his own payroll reports. At least for now, he had the time for it. As the business grows, that will be the first thing he lets go of.

The net savings was $1,850 the first year. ($2,900 - $500 - $550) After that, he would save $2,350 per year ($2,900 - $550).

Remember this is "after tax" money. It's a savings of taxes so it goes directly in his pocket.

The next year, his income almost doubled. So did his tax savings. He moved his sister and her husband into a house (from an apartment). They had a yard and more room for all of them. He bought himself a van he could drive himself.

I like to think about Alec's story when I hear from people that it's too hard to build a business. It's hard, but it's not too hard. There have been a lot of trailblazers who have left a trail for all of us to follow.

And with the tax savings he found, there was more money to use for his family and community and to build a nest egg for the future.

In the right situation, an S Corporation can be a powerful tool.

Discovering the Power of the C Corporation
A long-time client of mine met with me in early January 2018. She was concerned about what was going to happen with the Tax Cuts and Jobs Act. This was particularly true because she was a high income earner with her own professional services company and she lived in California.

She had dependents (elderly relatives) and an adult daughter who she supported. Since she lived in California, she had high property tax and high state income tax. She knew that she would lose most of those deductions, but hoped that the pass-through tax reduction would make up for the difference. I had the unenviable task of telling her that she wouldn't qualify for the pass-through tax reduction because her income was over the threshold and she had a service business.

Now what?

Secretly, I was happy that she was open to new ideas because there was a strategy that was going to work well for her. I'd mentioned it every year several times for years, but it always seemed like too much trouble.

She was now looking at an increase of $50,000 in taxes, so she was very open to changes.

The idea was to move some of the function of her business to a C Corporation. She had family members who could own the C Corporation so she could set up benefit plans that would be just for the benefit of her family. Otherwise, if she owned the C Corporation personally, she would need to include all of the employees of her other company on benefit plans.

One of the plans she wanted to put in place was a MERP (medical expense reimbursement plan). This allowed employees and directors of the company to cover all family medical expenses through the C Corporation. That made the expenses fully deductible.

Additionally, the income in the C Corporation was taxed at a maximum rate of 21%. Why a C Corporation? More benefits and lower tax rate add up to better strategy for a high income taxpayer in a high tax state post-2018.

There were implementation issues, of course. For example, the C Corporation needed a legitimate purpose for receiving income from the operating professional service company. There needed to be a contract for services, or at a minimum, a memo of understanding between the two entities. Plus, there needed to be an invoice and clear trail of the cash going in and out of the company. The C Corporation needs to have a real business purpose.

We had avoided typical C Corporation issues such as Personal Service Company (PSC), Personal Holding Company (PHC) and Excess Accumulated earnings. But she still needed to figure out how to pull the money out of the C Corporation. There would some salary for her family members who legitimately did work, benefits and then the rest would be loaned to investing LLCs that she owned.

She went from owing an extra $50,000 in 2018 (compared to 2017) and instead would now save $100,000 in 2018 (compared to 2017).

Will this strategy work for you? Maybe, if you have exactly the same set of circumstances. There are strategies that can work for just about anybody, just as long as everyone is clear that changes need to happen.

Throughout the book, we've looked at changes to your individual tax return, the benefits of properly setting up a business and 95 separate strategies. It only takes one of those, in the right circumstances to save you thousands of dollars in taxes.

The bonus you receive when you register your book is great, but it's nothing compared to the bonus the IRS is going to give you when you put these strategies to work for you.

Your $1,499 Bonus!
When you register your book at http://www.Taxmageddon2018.com/bonus/ with the password LessTaxNow, you're going to receive:

Access to the private forum for readers of Taxmageddon ONLY. Got a question? Ask it here.
Strategies with discussion points
Exclusive content you can use to further understand Insider's Tip
Notices as the law is further changed and refined
It costs you NOTHING to register. Do it today at http://www.Taxmageddon2018.com/bonus/.

Only you can determine what to do with this information. There will be winners and losers from the Tax Cuts and Jobs Act. The winners will adapt. The losers will complain. What will you do?

See you at the Insider's Circle.

Give This Link to Your Tax Professional!

TaxProsOnly.com

TaxProsOnly.com discusses ALL the Tax Law relating to the Trump Tax Plan and other topics discussed in the book. We'll talk about forms, reporting issues and all the changes that are bound to occur with this law.

It's just for Tax Pros. Why? It's boring, compliance stuff. We'll be talking about Tax Code, Treasury Regulations, Revenue Rulings, Revenue Procedures, IRS notices, Private Letter Rulings and Tax Court Cases. It's the stuff you WANT your Tax Pro to know.

Made in the USA
Middletown, DE
27 July 2018